THE LEADERSHIP FEED

DEVELOPING LEADERSHIP SKILLS FOR GEN-Z: A PRACTICAL GUIDE THROUGH SCHOOL AND COLLEGE ACTIVITIES

KRISHNA PRASAD NAGARAJ

For Raksha

Writing this dedication, I am overwhelmed with pride and a little bit of nostalgia … but mostly just panicking about how quickly you are growing up! You are about to be off to college and I can not wait for all the crazy adventures that await you. I kind of feel like grab some popcorn cos this is getting really serious!

From the late night cram sessions that quickly turned into snack fests all the way to full-blown celebrations of every single accomplishment (yes, even those ones where you just remembered to feed your dog) — witnessing this awe-inspiring person emerge has been quite a journey! I started writing this book on leadership inspired by the way that you can lead your own way through a high school drama-filled day of classes and hallways or survive family game nights, with style & sass – if nothing else from anyone elses perspective but definitely in an amazing illusionist dream state.

This book is full of wisdom, life advice and most likely some dad jokes to help you among the rest of the junior legends out in this wild world. May it arm you with some of the means to manage and fend off what is to come your way as well, possibly preventing a few missteps (like leaving that last slice for your roommate).

So, as you prepare for this monumental new phase, just know: I have your back forever; an astronomic amount of love crammed into my body and a chest full of "dad wisdom" to help guide the hell out from under everyone. Get out there and make this world your own- but remember to give the old man a call every once in a while (or send care packages)!

Contents

Introduction

Are you another one of those people out there who believes leadership is a kind of superpower you either have or don't, like some are just meant to lead. (And spoiler alert: that thinking is beyond over.) So whats the real tea? Winning nowadays requires us to improve and win over our own natural selves — become leaders starting with ourselves, and level up our leadership game.

Generation Z? The world is always changing, so we need to be led by those who can adapt and come up with ideas as quickly as the next iOS update, and who actually give a damn about their fellow person. The kind of leadership needed from us today is one that is flexible, innovative and kind

The best part? These are not superpowers, these are simply skills you can develop, with the right mindset, little practice and pinch of hustle. Are you ready to flex your leadership muscles? If so, this book is the key that you need for your future success. Let's do this!

Just barely, it will gently push you into the deep end if you are ready to move on. If so, this book is laughter and a confrontation in one!

Written for School and College students and peeps who just embarked upon the corporate journey, "Learn to

Lead: Developing Leadership Skills for Gen-Z" is a detailed book on how to build these essential skills during your early life in school and college. In this book, you will find useful information about how corporates works, real-life situations and lessons-learned that are applicable to the current context whether you are a high-school student dipping your toes into college for the first time or an university freshman trying to navigate club leadership or someone just interested in improving your own ability as a leader.

With a rapidly changing world and the continuing breakdown of traditional routes to leadership, you need to have breadth in your proficiency as a leader across different situations. This guide has you covered on an absolute range of topics, the learnings from basic forms of communication and conflict resolution, all through to perfecting delegation and team-building — everything an upcoming leader should know.

The book also delves into emotional intelligence, ethics and multicultural understanding — all things that count take on a key importance in our diverse, interconnected world today. You'll have a lot of opportunities to flex those skills —whether it's through school projects, extracurricular activities or community outreach— which means you're well-poised for all the challenges and opportunities coming your way.

As you move through the pages, be prepared for some practical yet useful thought-provoking exercises and reflective questions, which will be aimed at helping you internalise and apply what you learned. By reading until the end of this guide you will have grasped how a true leader leads and sets example, be surrounded by all the gear that those boss leaders possess, but also feel empowered to cut your own path of serving as a leader and make some effective changes in real life.

Alright then, let's proceed !

I

The Tea on Being a Boss

Understanding Leadership

It will be unfair to owe such a term entirely in one way, as Leadership is a big world and it is nearly impossible for all the traits related to leadership can only be defined in this definition. It is not just a work, or an identification... it is spirit, culture and dynamism that vibes deeply with you and also pulls everyone forward.

In my experience, leadership can crawl through the baffling colony and from a seemingly unlikely corner that you would not believe if it were not for the sake of genetics gone wrong.

Far from it, in fact quite the opposite; I believed leadership was about knowing everything and telling everyone else what to do. Still, over time I have discovered that the work of real leadership is more about asking good questions and listening. It is enabling those around you to feel appreciated for their work and encouraged to deliver at their best. That shift in thinking made me work differently and a better leader was born.

Relationships are the root of all leadership. Empowerment, not power over. Day 1 does start off with a big difference, though, as you can fend this off right away simply by changing your way of thinking slightly. There is trust, communication and shared identity which are foundational elements for collaboration and innovation but it requires a team/leadership to do so.

Among the most difficult, yet critically important essential roles of a successful leader is finding that elusive balance point between Vision and Reality. Otherwise, leaders need to be able to look past the present, ie sharing a vision of what-could-be on one hand and also practical in the ways of today. It takes a thoughtful head and an empathetic heart for this duality. It is about being willing to lay down a powerful vision that fires up and motivates the people you lead, while at the same time understanding what matters to them to their everyday challenges and aspirations.

From historical to present there are many styles of leadership as it does not have one definition. Leaders vary too, some being charismatic and extroverted or others more quiet and introspective. The Range varies from Hitler to Gandhi. What they have in common you might say is a credibility that connects with their followers. Authentic leaders should be more self-aware and transparent. They have learned who they are and are true to themselves, admitting faults without being ashamed. These traits lead to trust and loyalty, which are essential in successful leadership.

Another quality of successful leader is the tenacity to recover quickly from what might have seem like insurmountable failure. The reality is that bad things happen to good leaders consistently. What they do will define their legacy. Resilience implies a psychological adequate response to adversity, which includes learning from it and becoming better at it.

Despite some Ls, it's lit to keep a positive attitude and focus on the prize. The feeling of being able to get up again and recover from even the hardest of falls is a great motivator, and one that might inspire others to rise as well.

It takes a commitment to growth and an open mind. You gotta be willing to take risks and have fun with it! One should welcome the criticism as like has to be cool with feedback and critical reflection upon past action, and accept other opinions.

The journey through different levels of leadership continues to reveal that it is far bigger than the intellect. It is about building that human connection with people, knowing their dreams and obstacles, and then nurturing them all towards a shared vision. Leadership is a great responsibility but equally leadership is a great privilege.

In the course of the following chapters, I have tried to break it down into practical actions in a simple framework.

Every leader has it in them to make a lasting impact, not just on the organizations they lead, but on the lives of the people they touch. As Uncle Ben parker from Spiderman says " With great power, comes great responsibility"

Traits of a Leader

When you think about it in terms of the attributes we never tire of extolling in public discourse, leadership requires our energies below the level of attribute. Leadership is not having a title, forming command or even demanding respect. It is the complex concoction of various components working in harmony with each other to instigate, influence and lead others to an objective.

Leadership Archive: Keeping it Real

ARCHIVE (Adaptability, Resilience, Communication, Humility, Integrity, Vision and EQ)

Adaptability, which is quite a vibe. Leaders must adapt and remain open to new ideas and approaches in a fast changing landscape. They will change things up when needed and never shy away from some calculated risks. Leading in a way that is both on fleek and ahead of the game, capable of guiding their team through change with confidence and efficiency.

Another trait critical for any leader is resilience. In life as leaders will always encounter adversity and there will be times they get knocked back but it is their ability to bounce back from any setbacks that is so crucial. Resilient leaders stay positive, learn from failure and turn those setbacks into opportunities. Their fortitude allows them to handle the tough times but it also sets an example for their team that adversity can be faced using muscle all the way through.

Good communication is a must have for every leader. Propelling out and clearly communicating information, but also genuinely listen and quantifiably absorb feedback. Leaders who are able to communicate well forge better team relations, promote an environment of transparency and co-operation and also make it possible to get everyone supporting the organization's efforts. They do a great job of adapting their communication style for each unique audience, so when they speak ... others listen.

Humility is the quality that separates good leaders from great ones. They admit that they do not know and open up to what others have to offer. Gives credit where it is due, recognizes their team, isn't afraid to admit when they are wrong.

Integrity is the strongest underlying pillar of Leadership. This consistency in the practices, values and principles makes leaders of integrity cultivate the trust and respect of those under them. They are honest in their decision processes and take full responsibility for their distinction. The culture of trust always springs from their eternal commitment to transparency and ethical standards.

Vision is seriously such a leader key A. Specific and compelling Vision provides a clear target so everyone gets into the boat together and starts paddling in the right direction. And they communicate this vision with passion and clarity, energizing others to join the cause and collaborate in achieving it. Always plan a step ahead, predicting trends and problems, thus never hesitating to change its strategy for the better.

A major part of leadership is inner acumen. It involves the ability to be aware of, control, and express one's own emotions, and to handle interpersonal relationships judiciously and empathetically. Being able to handle interpersonal dynamics, emotional engagement and create an environment where everyone feels like they can be a significant part of the team is regarded as high EQ. How to do this: practice being an active listener, show understanding and empathy, and have a calming effect on others even when everything seems crazy.

In essence, a leader's vibes makes the ideal pick-and-mix of qualities that are ARCHIVE — adaptability, resilience, communication skills, humility, integrity, vision and emotional intelligence. And when these characteristics are exaggerated and lived out, they help our Leaders inspire, lead and conquer with their Squads.

Leaders vs. Managers

Leaders inspire you to chase your dreams; managers remind you to submit them by 5 PM!

Upon further reflection, differences between leaders and managers might appear on a spectrum of skills and approaches that characterize each role. Both are necessary for propelling an organization towards its end goals, but how they perform it and what their impact is, are poles apart.

Leadership usually starts with vision and inspiration. A leader has the habit of looking beyond small stuff and dreaming/climbing up at a very high scale. They are the dream-builders, daring to say "What if? and "Why not?" Viewing failure in this light is beneficial for global innovation and creates an atmosphere where creativity can blossom. Leaders are often the ones with responsibility to show direction and present a vision of where we need to go. They have proven themselves at understanding what drives and supports people, and they can turn a bunch of individuals into one cohesive team in no time.

Managers on the other hand are keepers of order and logic. They focus mostly on task execution and maintaining the system. Managers are good at organizing, planning and coordinating resources in order to ensure the project objectives within time, budget & quality. Typically, they have a high level of hands-on involvement making sure things get done. You see, managers love predictability and structure.

Leaders and managers can have a symbiotic relationship. A manager provides the pragmatic underpinning that a leader's vision needs to be turned into reality. Leaders may navigate the course, but it is managers that chart out the best route, each step measured and executed to perfection. The balance of this dynamic interplay is essential for any organization aiming to be both innovative and operationally excellent.

But the line between these two jobs is often blurry. Plenty of successful people possess both leadership and management characteristics. They infuse inspirational energy as well as make sure that the daily wheels are greased properly. This hybrid skill set is increasingly important in a rapidly evolving business climate where adaptability and agility are crucial.

In reflecting on my own past experiences this makes absolute sense — in fact, the best leaders I have come across nimbly switch between all of these roles depending upon what is required of them on that occasion. They know when to get out of the way, so their team can innovate and when to support with more structure and guidance. And only truly brilliant leaders achieve this.

Cultural context even may change what the required balance of leadership and management is for an organisation. For businesses in a more heavily regulated industry, the emphasis may be on management, with an eye toward compliance and risk management. However, in a start-up environment, leadership qualities might stretch further to vision setting, risk taking and change adaptability and embracing new technologies.

Ultimately, the notion that leaders and managers are different is not about the elevation of one over the other but understanding what each contributes. In an ideal situation, these two functions are interdependent, and the level of interaction between them can be key for an organization to perform effectively both in success as well as stability. Indeed the observer of these differences in themselves may learn a thing or two about how synergy can best be played out for anyone attempting to succeed in one or both of these roles.

The Role of Ethics

"Doing the right thing even when nobody is looking" - This may seem simple but need to be practiced so that its in-built in you.

But ethics can seem so far off in a world of vagueries, waffle and philosphising on paper. However, in the area of leadership, ethical alignment is the fundamental cause of trust, respect and successful leadership. It is the invisible thing that dictates actions, molds behavior and informs us of the vibes of our leaders and their team.

As we think about this dimension of ethics as leaders, it is helpful for us to remember that behaving ethically is not simply a matter of keeping the rules. This is about demonstrating principles that embody authenticity and honesty. Leaders who behave in an ethical manner make people feel Respected and listened to.

A fair and respectful attitude could maintain loyalty, encourage a positive environment and overall increase productivity.

Discuss the connection of ethical leadership to decision-making style. Every decision a leader takes will have ethical considerations, no matter how big or small. When it comes to where resources go, how conflict is mitigated and how team members are informed — an ethical code steers leader actions towards what is fair and equitable. Ethical leadership helps a leader to avoid being swayed by personal advantages and external pressures but they focus on what is best for everybody.

In addition, ethical leadership is not only concerned with what the leader does but also for nurturing an environment that promotes and rewards ethical behavior. This is done by setting and enforcing standards, training new squad members on ethical practices, and implementing checks to ensure this standard is being met. Team members are encouraged to do the right thing when they see that their leader does too. A shared belief in ethics can alter an organization, where every individual feels a part of something bigger than themselves.

No matter what leadership role you find yourself in, ethical dilemmas are guaranteed to rear their head.

These moments are the ones that determine the kind of leader you really are. Adversities, such as these times, bare the need of a good strong moral base. In these and similar situations, leaders must exercise discretion while showing courage in their decision-making by balancing the consequences with the interests of all parties concerned. Transparent communication and open mindedness, not exclusively hearing about divergent perspectives, but actually listening to them can at least result in an integrity-retainable solution to ethical dilemmas.

When we think of historical and current examples of leadership, it is most notable that those who are remembered by the masses were people who lead with strong ethical values.

It is really a fast-paced competitive world, in the race of reaching to the top very often you forget about the importance which Ethics hold in order to be successful. However, real leadership is achieved not only in the fact that it boldly goes where no human has dared go before, but in how it gets there. Being obsessed with principle is what paves the way for trust, relationships that last and yes, sustainable success. They know that they are setting an example in what they do and what they leave behind will be their legacy, taking the high road, even at great cost to themselves.

But when it comes to one's own leadership trajectory, I have learned that this means engaging in a measured constant re-examination of what one believes and acts on. This realization and determination towards morality ensure personal development as well as the betterment of the whole organization. And by placing ethics at the heart of how they operate, leaders can bring about lasting change that outlasts their own professional achievements and strengthens a culture of integrity to provide for the common good.

Leadership in Everyday Life

Mastering the Art of Not Losing It Before Your Morning Coffee!

Life goes on as we work our way through the daily grind, and leadership is not exclusive only to debates and epic sports and boardroom battles. It's omnipresent in our daily human interactions, subtly shaping how we connect with each other, form decisions and motivate the others around us. Everyday leadership is about identifying the opportunities to lead that happen in our everyday lives, and then going out there and seizing them with intention (and some empathy too).

Picture your morning scramble and how the craziness from getting ready can also cause added stress, otherwise know as....frustration. Leadership ... in this case patience and order. Established in a soothing manner with rhythm and consideration for the needs of everyone involved, resourceful morning practices ensure the start of every new day with minimal friction. So, by you know, keeping it laid back, following a steady routine, and being aware of all emotions involved can really easily help turning a potentially chaotic day into a nice chill morning. This is not about controlling things, it's more of leading the way with purpose and empathy.

Leadership is not reserved for the privileged few on a specific floor. It manifests in the ways we work with teammates, treat support staff and cultivate a culture of happiness. In this context everyday leadership is not being aggressive or dominating, it means stepping forward, offering solutions instead of whinging about problems and noticing stand-out contributions by others. With mutual respect and gratitude along with cheering, you can set a culture of everyone feeling important and inspired to be the best-version or themselves.

The community – leadership can range from coordinating a local neighborhood clean up to volunteering at your food shelter. There, these acts of service offer evidence of caring for others and call for collective effort to seek common goals. It is more about having a vision that goes beyond oneself and then doing one's small bit towards creating something positive. Through this type of leadership, we are able to make stronger and coherent communities in which people feel they can be meaningful.

Indeed, even in casual interludes leadership exerts its influence. For coordinating a night out or the next family holiday and as maybe even more importantly for hosting dinner parties. In a social setting, leadership would involve having an eye for what others like and want to talk about, causing everyone to feel welcomed in the conversation, and resolving any conflicts that may arise. Though they seem small, these are moments that sharpen the skills needed to lead in big scenarios.

Contemplate on self-growth and leadership. This requires creating objectives, constraints, and holding one accountable to their bidding. We've taken to the notion that it is more of growing thorns resiliently when we are put into tough situations and always finding ways to be stronger. If we become effective leading ourselves, then we will leave an invisible template for us that further enables our leader within us when in broader leadership contexts.

When it comes to our everyday lives and how we interact with our friends/loved ones, leadership is characterized in making them trust you, support them through their weak points and be that source of strength when needed most. It is about active listening, giving advice as necessary and sometimes only being there. But such are the precious head-and-heart bonds that can be waiting when a leader cares for him or herself and in turn bridges into care for others — via empathy, integrity, genuine concern.

Leadership in Everyday Life - The really interesting thing I discovered is that everyday leadership has nothing to do with grand gestures or coming up with the next command ushered down from above. It's all those little things which often go unremarked that add up to make the difference. It is the awareness of our effect on those around us and making that impact a positive one. As we adopt these standards, then we improve not only ourselves but also motivate others to lead with grace and equip talent around.

Put it to practice - 1

Leadership at Home : Reach the heart through the stomach, the art of ordering from a Food Delivery App.

1. Understand each members diet restrictions and likes and disliked - Probing & Active Listening

2. Pick a day and add items to the cart

3. Communicate that you will be ordering the list to seek feedback

4. Execute flawlessly

5. Repeat until they come to you one day and say 'What are we having today?'

II

Finding your Leadership Vibe

Self-Assessment Techniques

One of the steps in becoming a great leader is to look within oneself. One thing that I am learning is that leadership, as much guiding others as it is about self-knowledge. Sitting on your mat is like a walk towards knowing yourself, it's impossible to lead if one has not experienced anything. This is where self-assessment techniques come in handy as tools to reveal different layers about what makes us who we are. They help us identify what we are good at, where our trouble areas lie, and how we impact the people around us.

By examining your strengths, weaknesses, opportunities, and threats, you get the full scoop on where you are at right now.

Strengths highlight what we do well, what sets us apart, what makes us unique, and where we totally kill it. These are the qualities and skills that have brought us success in the past. Weaknesses, on the other hand, reveal areas where we may catch some Ls, where we need improvement, and where we might face challenges. Opportunities pop up as outside factors that we can use to our benefit, while Threats are just those obstacles that could seriously drag us down and stop us from leveling up.

Strengths	Weakness
Opportunity	Threats

Pencil down the above box and keep it as reference.

360 Degree feedback is another good tool to use. This process consists of feedback from different sources -peers, juniors, teachers and even self-feedback. As an outcome, you receive a balanced perspective of our behavior and capability. This holistic approach can reveal things you never even knew you neglected. This allows you to compare your actions and allows for informed adjustments.

Tools like Myers-Briggs Type Indicator (MBTI) or Big

Five Personality Traits help us to know more about our basic person and how we are likely to respond. Knowing your vibe can help you to understand how its vibing with other or choosing any stuff or reacting to a situation. Google this up and take up the test, you will know your Type!

These tests can be especially helpful in determining communication tactics, problem-solving techniques and leadership styles.

Another self-evaluation device that is profoundly successful is reflective journaling. Each time we write about our lived experiences, thoughts, or feelings its like intentionally bringing introspection to the table. Journaling — To document progress and track growth over time, identify recurring patterns of behavior, gain clarity on goals and aspirations. This is a self-reflective dialogue — One that helps you know yourself better and grow every day.

Self-assessment — Mindfulness practices, such as meditation and self-reflection also have a large role in self-assessment. We also become more in tune with what we are thinking and feeling by cultivating Mindfulness. This heightened awareness allows you to navigate life with more clarity and intention as we respond to the situations around us. Mindfulness invites us to witness our reactions, without judgment, allowing for greater understanding of our typical responses and unconscious intentions.

In practicality, it could also mean putting on your headphones and listening to something you love for 8 minutes!

Self-reflection is something that is not a task fit to be done once, but a lifestyle. It takes a willingness to be honest and open, as well as a readiness to look at things head-on that make you squirm. The information you gain from these methods is only as useful as the response we employ. We set ourselves the personal challenge of self-assessment and in doing so become better leaders.

While you still experiment and develop your self-assessment methods, it is important to acknowledge that there will never ever be perfection; the target is always continual enhancement. The last thing I want to remind new leaders about, and what will be a universal reminder for all of us at every level regardless of tenure, is that leadership is not a destination — it's a journey. It means self-assessment isn't an audit we take once and then hang on the wall as proof we're good enough to deserve the title. When we take the time to really understand our own selves, we lead others with more integrity, empathy and belief.

Identifying Strengths and Weaknesses

Acknowledging our ability from inability is the first step in the long road to become a successful Leader. This can only happen with profound self-contemplation and a true open view of our strengths and weaknesses. Recognizing your traits helps you to be more relaxed and at ease in leadership, so that you are better prepared to contribute to yourself and people around you.

Start looking back on your experiences. Think of times you have been more or less successful. What skills were going to save you in those times? How did your peers, mentors or people who reported to you respond? Such reflections really help to understand your natural strengths and some areas that you can work on. You should take an open and unfazed attitude to this exercise as well — do not mind compliments or corrections.

Another good approach to gauge strengths and areas is through assessments and feedback tools. Personality tests, leadership assessments, and 360-degree feedback surveys can provide you with an objective data point for both your style of leading and how effective that is. There are a dime and dozen on the internet to get your spoof. Such tools help to reveal patterns and tendencies that might not be clear with self-reflection alone. Nevertheless, these results must be seen through a critical lens and are one part of a larger self-assessment.

Also, having someone mentor you or work with a coach can be very helpful! They can give you some insights as to what others see about your leadership and advice on how to get better in it. They can give you advice on how to capitalize on your strengths and hedge against your weaknesses. Discussions with a mentor can also keep you accountable and driven towards continuous improvement.

Remember too that you can learn a lot by simply observing other people. Observe how individuals in leadership position are at their strength or sideline. What traits do you see in them that you would like to have? Find out what they are doing wrong which you can learn from. In this book, you will discover what true leadership is by learning from the examples of other great leaders who have made it and those that clearly crashed out.

This is where the rubber hits the road... so to speak; in other words, now you know what your strengths/weaknesses are, it's time to build a plan. Find ways to use your strengths as much as you can. This will not only make you a more effective leader, but it will make you feel even better about your position and knowledge in the field. While your strength, at the same time work on your weaknesses. For some, this might mean getting more training and experience in areas you are less-than confident in, outsourcing tasks that lie too far outside your area of expertise for comfort, or just being honest with yourself about when to hop off the bull.

So what this ultimately leads us to as a conclusion, is the fact that strengths and weaknesses are a moving target and they are never a one time figure. Experience and effort could help them evolve... Ongoing personal and professional development comes by continually re evaluating your self-assessment and adjusting your development plan accordingly. The field of leadership is a fluid pursuit, which requires continual adaptability and self-awareness if one is to realize success over the long term.

It is an ongoing process of recognizing and understanding your strengths and weaknesses. It takes hard work, being real and constant evolving. But by going through this process, you can emerge as a better leader—better at listening, empathizing, and handling challenges in the most ethical way.

Establishing Some Lit Personal Goals

In my first job, when my boss asked me what did I want to become, I without an ounce of humility said 'I want to become the General Manager of the company'. It was a BHAG - Big Hairy Aggressive Goal!

I think the point about setting personal goals is one of leadership fundamentals. This journey of transformation into a leader is full of goals and the will to accomplish each one with success. Personal goals serve as a compass, helping us navigate the difficult terrains of leadership and keeping us on track.

First thing first when you are setting personal goals is that you have to know what your own strengths and weaknesses. The self-awareness is critical. Understand what we are good at and work on that, understand where we struggle and build practical step-by-step plans.

For example, a goal could be to take a course or do frequent practice on public speaking if that is where you need help. These introspective processes efficiencies goal setting, growth mindset; both of which are necessary for a leader.

Another key factor — articulating goals with granularity. Vague or general goals make you wonder wtf because there are so many options. Rather, goals should be SMART — specific, measurable, achievable, relevant and time-bound. For instance, instead of a loosely defined goal to hone "communication skills," one may insist on "signing up for an effective communication workshop by the end of this quarter and inculcating its learning in team meetings". This clarity on actionable goals highlights a growth path, after achieving which one can measure their progress in turn.

And y'know, like, tbh, it is like really important to ensure that your own goals totally vibe with the leadership vision and values of the org or team you are running. This alignment ensures that personal development contributes to collective success. There is a sense of purpose as well as motivation when there are personal and organizational goals in sync. Leaders who lead with their own personal growth and how it benefits the squad as a whole are usually way more inspiring and effective.

The regular strolls and workshops for goal-setting are crucial as well. Leadership is one such constantly evolving activity and there can be constant changes in the demands and requirements. Review the goals every so often, and make adjustments with time. Reflection on progress, keeping the big picture in perspective and celebrating successes gives an added boost to stay positive and proactive with goal setting.

We all know how important accountability is for working on personal goals. Having a mentor, coach or another trusted colleague to share goals with can give you additional support and motivation. These are the people who can provide insightful feedback, and help us stick to our objectives in a manner that is much more accountable. This outsider view can also be instrumental in helping us to see our own blind spots and bring new perspectives into our goal-setting.

But last, least is the ability to be agile and tough. Rarely do personal goals fall in a straight line. You will have challenges and setbacks but these will become the place you should learn your most valuable lessons. Holding onto these with some perseverance and the ability to contort can result in challenges not as a setback but instead as growth. Leaders who can pass through these challenges resolutely but gracefully find themselves more seasoned and better prepared.

Looking back at our attempt to create personal goals, we see it as a long and ongoing process. In doing so, leaders build their own skills and help to motivate and uplift others. Personalized goal setting has more to do than personal accomplishment, it is part of a greater vision where you can influence change.

Building Confidence

Confidence is a bit like learning to dance — first, you are awkward and stepping on toes but before long, you are moonwalking through life!

Confidence is considered by many to be a characteristic you either have or do not. As I sit here and reflect back on my experiences, it has become extremely apparent that confidence is not a condition you either have or not. Confidence is actually a skill that can be developed much like learning to play the guitar — invested time and nurturing through perfection of your art will follow. Realizing this has been a quite transformative enlightenment through my journey of leadership.

Doubting myself Filled self-doubt When I first took a leadership role I doubted myself, my capabilities and couldn't deal with the possibility of screwing up all things. But the more I went through challenges, the more I saw: confidence comes from doing. Every little win, every crisis averted, and every hard conversation had slowly built up my self belief.

And it is an important thing to realize that confidence does not mean never feeling unsure; it means knowing you. _. are tough enough to deal with whatever life throws at you. It was my game changer mindset. I changed my mindset and started to see challenges as chances for development rather than threats to my capableness. With this mindset I was able to handle challenging situations entering them with a question and solution seeking attitude rather than dread.

Preparation is another key part of growing our confidence. I have an unforgettable memory of a presentation that felt like it was going to bury me with anxiety when I was just starting out. Just the idea of getting up in front of a room full of industry veterans made me sweat. But I had spent hours preparing, practicing my speech and thinking what questions would be asked. All the prep paid off when the day finally came! I gave my presentation with poise, and the great feedback I received did a lot for my self-esteem.

Requesting feedback has been crucial to my gaining of confidence. While difficult at times, all the constructive criticism has been beneficial. It has allowed me to improve on the areas where I am lacking, and it provided me with a clear path for my development. Even better, the pats on the back for my work made me feel like I was doing something right and kept me coming back to do more.

Another pillar that has contributed to my confidence is the support from mentors and peers. Being around people who see the potential in me has been so empowering. Time and time again, their words of encouragement have been the extra nudge to get me out of my comfort zone and make me take more risks. As I look back on these memories, I understand how important it is to develop a network of support as a leader.

During times of lower confidence, I have been reminded to think about achievements from the past. I have never had a perfect memory — so tracking accomplishments, however small, is proof of what I can do. This has been largely helpful when I am trying to tackle new (and scary) things. As I remember how far I have come, it gives me the courage to move forward with a greater assuredness.

Confidence is a constant build up. It is a hard-enough task of committing to be better, and outside of my comfort zone, not to mention the will power that allows me to fail but yet pushing on. When I look back now, it becomes clear that with every win and failure along my own journey has worked to shape me in some way as a leader. Confidence is not a place, it's not the bridge between two theme parks; welfare and perceived welfare. Confidence is alive inside of you. Confidence is a living being that lives within your leadership. And so, in my ever-evolving journey of self-discovery and growth, I continue to work on this priceless characteristic — recognizing that it is the key which will unlock the door to courageous, authentic leadership for me.

Seeking Feedback

A rouge might say "Don't ask my opinion if you can't handle the truth". Funny, the truth is that feedback is one of the most powerful weapon a leader can have.

In effect, this monument holds up a mirror onto the actions, decisions and human cost of it all. As leaders, we can all become so enamored with our vision and strategy and plans that we inadvertently forget the value of an outside perspective. But feedback loops are about more than just gathering perspectives on our own work–they exist to create an ethos of transparency and growth and respect.

I remember my early days as an inexperienced leader & feeling cautious to solicit feedback. It felt... exposed, like I was revealing a weak spot or something — can you relate? In time, I came to understand that it is this very vulnerability which not just strengthens a leader. This gave me permission to gather feedback and explore the strengths, weaknesses, biases I have become acutely aware of previously unabated blind spots in my leadership.

As a starting point, feedback starts with building a culture where team members trust that the environment is safe for them to express their thoughts openly. This takes trust — established over time, by feedback being received with an open if not gleeful mind, reinforced by actual development. In order to properly do that, one of the more effective method to set an example. Active listening to feedback by leaders shows the team that their voices are heard.

Constructive feedback should be specified, fact-based and achievable. This is a bit different than saying,

"You need to communicate better," which comes off pretty vague when compared to, "Your points in the last meeting were clear but the team felt there was no space for discussion." The first is just a theory, the second gives you a real-world scenario and a roadmap. In the process of receiving feedback, having an open mind, actively listening, asking for elaborations, and taking time to reflect without getting defensive is really important.

A leader can further illustrate that feedback is not welcome by his or her reaction to it and make the chances of receiving enough feedback slim to none. Thank you for the feedback and I appreciate it — the mere act of having a conversation like this, explaining how feedback can be actioned means you are committed to growing. Feedback, Transcript, Follow-up Implementing suggested changes and showing the outcomes can add to it because assuming a team member says something results, it would go on push-loop and start creating a more promising and dynamic team environment.

In general, feedback should not be limited to a one-time event. Feedback is a continual conversation. Scheduled check-ins, anonymous surveys and open forums may serve as checkpoints for team members to sound off. It is also good to ask for feedback in a number of places like peers, mentors, and even clients. All in all, each perspective can provide valuable insights into improving leadership practices.

Its equally important to reflect on the feedback you receive. The process includes reviewing the information, identifying trends and making connections to how this can be incorporated into a leadership style. This virtuous loop of soliciting, accepting, digesting and implementing feedback nurtures self-improvement skills that ultimately result in better leaders who understand the human aspect of things.

In the end, being willing to receive feedback speaks volumes about how passionate a leader really is for excellence...and how humble they are as well. It recognizes that leadership is an arm and a leg, but it is a practice in which you learn, tune into things, and evolve. Keeping this focused approach to valuing feedback makes it easier for leaders to navigate the complexity of the role with clarity and impact, inspiring the team in a way that meaningful collective success is achieved.

III

Learning Through School Projects

Choosing Projects: Because 'This Could Be a Disaster' Isn't a Vibe!

It quickly becomes apparent, when reflecting upon the path to effective leadership, was selecting the right projects. For an individual, this outwardly simple decision could define the course of your career; for the team, it may even determine whether they find their dominant strength and reach escape velocity — i.e. a whole lot hangs in the balance. If it were just a matter of grabbing titles off the board, there isn't really any thought to be had in that so much as there would be consideration for what or who you are supporting — which is not small fries either, but rather sidestepping the actual point to consider which group might benefit more.

IPL Auctions: The "Choose Your Battles" Principle

Ever seen an IPL auction? It's like a leadership nightmare wrapped in a goldmine of opportunity. Players are bidded on as if they're tech startups, while captains and coaches sit on the sidelines, sweating over their next recruit.

Will this player fit our culture? Is he worth the money? Can I even pronounce his name? Leaders are always making tough decisions. But in the IPL, sometimes you also have to deal with decisions like "Chris Gayle or the budget to feed the entire team for a month?"

Lesson: A great leader knows how to pick battles. Sometimes, the biggest star isn't the best fit for your culture (or your wallet). Don't get dazzled by the highest price tag—invest in the talent that aligns with your vision and is ready to deliver on the ground.

Each project you work on should be in alignment with personal and professional goals. If the project that you undertake is aligned well with your own values and aspirations, then it will naturally draw out only the best in you. A project which supports the strategic aims of the organisation or institution is more likely to attract support (and resources if it is needed), and hence be more successful. That connection ensures that both the individual and organization benefit from each other.

Yet alignment is not the whole story. Evaluate the idea and calculate its feasibility, ROI etc. This includes an analysis of the resources, time and skill sets needed.

A good project quickly becomes a micro burden for your team, if it requires more than the tool can provide or if it needs from teamentities more than they have. This ability to balance vision with pragmatism is a critical leadership skill that needs to be honed so as to pick projects that are not only aspirational but also do-able.

A second key metric is the opportunity for personal and team growth. The projects that defy the norm and go beyond simply making aesthetic play-offs, are typically those which result in groundbreaking advancements. The projects provide encouragement for innovation, resilience and a culture of improvement going forward. Leadership is a teaching-and-learning scenario: leaders select project that allow the team to learn and develop.

Risk is part of any project — how a leader handles this risk can determine the difference between success and failure. It is one of the most important thing in a project to judge both risks and rewards well enough so that neither we end up with less profit margin in the worst case scenario nor it costs double time by overestimating it. A wise leader will consider these variables and balance by selecting which projects have risk-reward ratio to stick their skip out and what are the tact that can control this hazard.

Teamwork is yet another element in decision making. Engage in discussions with your team members and other stakeholders to hear their insights and perspectives as well, and get a deeper sense of just what the project could be. This collaboration involves everyone, which not only results in better decision-making but also creates a sense of ownership and responsibility among the team. People who feel like their voice is heard will be more likely to put skin in the game via either code contributions or additional funds.

And it's also essential to understand that not all projects are equal. Suggested steps to take: hands-off, or more involved leadership It allows the leader to ascertain and align their leadership style with the nature of the project so that the leadership styles are effective in managing a project.

It turns out that questioning the experiences that have gone before can provide good lessons. Taking a look at prior projects, whether they are successes or failures can tell you about what works and what doesn't. Reflecting on what happened and why, the good, bad and worst band- Factors involvedThis reflective practice helps leaders to make better decisions avoiding mistakes done in past and repeat success stories.

Ultimately, it all boils down to finding the right projects, and that is really about combining practical reality with strategic foresight forcing up into light on our own shadow strategy. Through thoughtful consideration of alignment, feasibility, growth potential, risk, the importance of growing one's network and experience and past learning experiences leaders can make decisions that put them on a path of personal growth and organizational success.

Team Collaboration

A red-hot sense of Teamwork Collab is a key attribute for any aspiring leader. From personal experience, I remember the countless work we pulled off that wasn't a result of any one person's genius mind but was solely because of a dope, solid team.

In these times we know the heart and soul of leadership — when not issuing orders but enabling an arena to be one where every voice is heard and every voice carries equal worth.

One of the biggest lessons I have learned very early into my career is that trust is an extremely critical factor in a team. When Trust Erodes, Collaboration Dissolves. Collaboration without the trust upon which it is built is a thin covering that turns brittle at the first touch of conflict. It is only through a transparent and vulnerable place, we can begin this building of trust. Personal stories, fallibility, and vulnerability all have a role to play in breaking down walls and establishing an atmosphere where team members feel secure and valued. At the heart of any powerful collaboration, is this sense of psychological safety.

The Grandfather of the cornerstones that make up team collaboration is listening. Active listening is more than just hearing words; it means that we also understand their underlying emotions or intentions. I remember this one instance where a team member was going through a personal issue, and it reflected in the way they were working. I listened to their struggles and reassured them when they missed deadlines. That gesture of empathy not only solved the immediate problem but also united our team as it created a much easier field to work with moving forward.

A team being diverse is like a two sided coin. You get some cool view points and wisdom on one hand, but some dramas and clashing of ideas on the other both which has pros and cons. Acknowledging difference is not enough to embrace diversity — you have to actively seek and value diverse points of view. Creating an environment where every team member believes they can bring their unique insights to the table has helped in generating fresh ideas and enhances collaboration.

Communication is important so that everyone can understand and be on the same page. Which means, not only should one be articulate in expressing what they are thinking but also set these expectations and feedback on a regular. We had a daily check-in system for progress and impediments for example in one project each team member would share their experiences very briefly. It goes a long way to keep everyone in the same loop and answer questions as they arise, which makes everything more efficient.

Hype and props up every teams work no matter what. Noticing the achievements, minor and brutal, generates a feeling of gratitude and enhances the inspiration to work more cohesively in a team. I remember one project in particular where we hit roadblock after roadblock, but we kept joyfully celebrating every little victory — no matter how small — and our spirits stayed high until one day when everything finally clicked into place.

True leadership as it relates to team collaboration is not ruling with an iron fist but nailing the collective leverage. It is about cultivating a place where every member of the team feels they have space enough to put their best foot forward. Looking back at my journey, the projects that were most successful are the ones where we all came together to own it and be proud of our work.

Collaboration of teams is not static act its a Dynamics process Alway going until the project gets completed. This is something that needs to evolve and change with our thoughts in an ongoing basis. Leaders who build teams methodically through the creation of trust, active listening, pushing diversity, clear communication and celebration of success are destined to form a collaborative culture where teams flourish and unlock staggering achievements.

Role Assignment

Knowing team dynamics is crucial for Leadership success. Role Assignment-The most important part of all this is roles assignment. Looking back at what made me successful, I have learned that role assignment is not a job rather an art that requires careful thought, empathy and a keen understanding of the bigger picture. "You can't get a fish to climb a tree" choose the right people for the role they can succeed in.

For most of my journey as a leader, I have found it difficult to assign roles. Allocating the immediate to the willing, rather than to the most able. However, often this method was frustrating and ineffective. I did not really learn the importance of carefully selecting roles for your team which can make or break moral and productivity until after several mistakes.

One of the first lessons I was taught is understanding the strength and weaknesses of each team member as an individual. But it goes beyond a simple skill set and becomes mired in understanding what drives each person, wants from their career, and their strengths as a worker. One example I remember: a project where I put a careful planner in an immediate, fast-decision role. This mismatch was palpable, and it wasn't until I reorganized the roles to put my planner in a position where they were playing to strength that we made any substantial progress.

Role assignment should also help instill a feeling of ownership and responsibility. Team members who believe their roles are lining up with what they do best and enjoy doing will behave with a sense of initiative, and responsibility. I saw this so clearly in a team that I led in the past- every person had their autonomy to design their role, grounded on what they were good at. What this resulted in was a tight unit where every person on our team was driven, and making a real impact towards our shared goals.

In addition to this, role assignment is not an activity that occurs only once but should be practiced as a continued process. Teams grow up and people too. I later realized more reflective of another long term project, and how as the project was evolving roles had to be reconsidered. This flexibility helped us to be more adaptable in the face of change and encourage continued high levels of engagement and efficiency.

Communication is the key in this process. Frequent communication ensures everyone is aware of roles and expectations and reduces the chance of miscommunications. I can recall an instance where ambiguity around roles resulted in countless tasks being completed more than once and deadlines going unmade. This was an important learning for establishing the importance of clear communication and having timely check-ins so that roles are maintained to be well defined as informed.

Recognize that not all roles are shiny but they represent an important piece to the whole puzzle. By learning to value the work of everyone — including those honeybees at the back — we can build a culture where all small contributions are celebrated. Some of the best teams I have observed are those where those behind the scenes work whether it coordinating, ensuring that everyone understands what is expected or just doing the incredibly dull receptionist role — were celebrated and appreciated which added to a feeling of harmony and motivation throughout the team.

In looking back at these experiences, it is clear that assigning roles is a complex, ever shifting part of leadership. That is the delicate balance of strategic foresight and an empathetic angle. When done well, leaders can help their teams realise the full scope of what they are capable of achieving as a team — which motivates performance, satisfaction and growth. It is why role assignment is more than an administrative housekeeping and a foundational leadership skill.

Conflict Resolution

'Of Cats and Dogs' - Leading through conflict is the storm on the ocean that will always be apart of leadership. Continuing to write, and by reflecting on my own experiences, I understand conflict as more than just an obstacle but rather an opportunity to grow and gain deeper perspective. This would be a time of stress where real leadership is forged.

I spent a lot of the beginning of my career seeing conflict as failure, an indication that something was deeply wrong. If I could not evade it I would hope that some kind of alchemy within me, or between us, might make it disappear completely... but if not — then there we were in a heated showdown. It turns out that both strategies, I discovered the hard way, were pretty ineffective. Avoidance led to festering problems, and confrontation without empathy only escalated things. It took me a while to believe and to understand the power of conflict resolution is in the why as opposed to the what induced rhetoric.

A disagreement with a colleague about the direction of an important project was a defining moment for me along my path. Initially I wanted to jump in and prove my point, sure in how right I was. But, as the war rolled on, it was obviously that my approach was driving a wedge between us. I stood back and listened closer. I found that from a different place, my colleague viewpoint was completely legitimate and had observations and concerns which I had not noticed etc. What I learned from this is that listening comes not just hearing words, but in getting the feeling and motive behind it.

One of the funny things about conflict resolution is you have to strike a balance between being too empathetic and being too assertive. Fat chance it is all about the room in which everyone has their say and gets listened to and so do you, as long as you know your own self — of course. The balance is difficult to find in high-stress scenarios, but extremely important in maintaining a culture where everyone trusts each other and works as a team.

One of the kind of best techniques that I have found is to respond with active listening. That means not simply listening to what the other person has to say, but really taking in their words — identifying their emotions and asking open questions to make sure you understand the full story. One of the things doing this is to 'cool' emotions, it also shows respect and allows for openness which are essential when working on building trust.

Yet what appears to be an even greater skill is being able to control your own feelings. Fighting usually makes me want to defend myself, react defensively or become upset. But you, as their leader, must stay calm and rational. This is not about controlling your feelings, but understanding them and managing them. Things like practicing mindfulness and deep-breathing work well on a daily basis to help keep you emotionally sane.

We also need to keep centered on the issue and not necessarily take the conflict personally. It only further divides us when we take to attacking someone's character or questioning their motives. The key is to not make it about your intentions (good or bad) as the messenger. Instead, focus on the specific behaviors or decisions and what short term impact they have (positive or negative). This helps keep the conversation constructive and solution-based.

Looking back on them now, I see conflict not as anything to be worried about, but rather as an opportunity for innovation and growth. As long as you approach them with empathy and sensitivity, conflicts can provide greater understanding, deeper connections and ultimately superior outcomes. This is something we have to keep learning and improving upon with time, humility, and personal growth.

Leadership is not conflict avoidance; it is conflict conquest. It is about converting moments of tension into moments of bonding and growth. We see that conflict is not just an issue to resolve but a part of the development process of leadership.

Evaluating Success

"Operation success, but patient died" - Success is often the real direction to the compass in the moving field of leadership. However, success is more complex than that metric alone, not solely tangible or numerical. True leadership reflects reflecting, adapting, and growing; a judgment of success that requires scale.

Realize the possibilities of how success can look like. Be it in team members development or forming a collaborative culture, or reaching a common goal. Such qualitative elements are typically beyond the ossified world of traditional metrics, but are certainly fundamentals. But if we want a shared understanding of the implications our leadership has, we will have to look far deeper than that and recognize the underlying strems that drive development.

A key method is to ensure that you consistently practice self-reflection. We are doing a better job of evaluating our decisions—both the outcomes of decisions and, increasingly, the processes and interactions that informed those decisions. Did we make any decisions that were exclusionary? Did we create the environment where others could be proactive in contributing their best efforts? These questions are what allow us to measure the more elusive, but no less crucial aspects of success.

Another precious weapon is the feedback you receive from others. Feedback from peers, mentors and team members is a support as when someone shows the mirror to them they get an insight back. It provides a wake-up call to where we are blind and need to do better. It can be a great force for good, but only if feedback-prone to common dysfunctions is no longer appropriate. By showing that they are willing to listen and learn, leaders establish a norm for betterment.

In addition, sometimes the telltale signs are quite a resilient and flexible team or not. How does the team deal with adversity? Effective leadership is displayed when we are able to meet adversity head-on and find new paths through it. Actually, it says to me that there is a lot of sustainability built into the foundation that makes this turbulence possible to navigate in, relatively new programmers even taking the reins — and it also feels empowering.

The congruence between one's values and the companies values is focusing on being a success meter. People trust and follow leaders who are authentic, lead with integrity. When you live true to what is espoused, you will foster a more cohesive group and people will be united in their purpose. This synchronisation is not always easy to maintain but it's required for long-lasting success.

True leadership is not just a function of the present but ensuring that future generations can own this notion. What matters isn't success, but the leaders we build, the authority we instill and the good we do. This anticipatory outlook allows us to rise above instant profits and look into sustained solutions.

"Sometimes you win, Sometimes you Learn" - Measuring success in leadership ends up being a complicated, perennial struggle. And thus, it is a mix of introspection and external feedback, tinged with clear-eyed realism about both the tangible and intangible results that must be balanced. It's about realizing that leadership is not an endpoint; it is a never-ending progression towards becoming better and doing more. It is with this human approach we can endeavor to lead from the heart, encouraging purpose and compassion in our purposeful way of living.

IV

Leadership in Sports

The Captain's Role

Put yourself in your college graduation glory—standing on the field (or court, or whatever your sport is) staring out at the competition like you were about to put up the most legendary play ever. Except this time what lies in front of you is a chaotic blend of opportunity and pure chaos — more stressful than finals week, with a little less sweat but even fewer jitters). But as a captain, you're not the person with the armband or the one shouting "Let's go!" during warmups. You have some serious responsibilities—gassing up your team when they are losing, making sure no one is beefing in practice, and reminding the squad to concentrate on next, while the other half are thinking about what they are going to do after the practice.

Being a sports captain? It is simply to be great at the game. You have to read your squad with that emotional intelligence — knowing when they need you to give them a little pep talk or just shut up with the memes and inside jokes. And ethical fortitude? That's sports code for "don't be a glory hog, pass the ball and try not to skip the team bonding pizza nights."

Whether you are helping lead the team to a championship or just trying not be 15 minutes late to practice, every captain is a leader, protector and motivator for their collective squad — not to mention he/she makes sure nobody at anytime forgets the team handshake.

"Nobody is great at everything" - Leadership Starts with Awareness of Self. A captain has to know what he or she is good at and where he or she will be weak, because their actions will have a tail-whip behind it for the rest of a crew. With that self-awareness, a captain leads from an authentic position; it supports the consistent effort to create an environment in which everyone feels seen and heard. It is the self-knowledge that allows the captain to chart not only the waters of their team but also intimately familiar with all emotional seas they must cross!

The Captaincy Carousel: 'Dhoni vs. Kohli' Dilemma

Cricket teaches us one vital lesson: No matter how hard you try, you'll never make everyone happy. If you're leading a team like the Indian cricket team, expect comparisons to be your constant companion.

Remember when people debated endlessly about who's the better captain—MS Dhoni or Virat Kohli?

You know you've achieved true leadership when your subordinates are passionately critiquing your style at every chai break. Dhoni, the cool cucumber, and Kohli, the aggressive tiger.

Lesson: Leadership isn't one-size-fits-all. Sometimes you need to be the zen master like Dhoni—calm in the chaos. Other times, you've got to be Kohli and light a fire under your team to get them moving. Pick your leadership style like you'd pick your Powerplay strategy—based on the opponent and the situation!

Another critical factor in the Captain's role is decision-making. When waters are rough, prompt decisions can be everything and the difference between safety and disaster. Yet these decisions are rarely so simple moments in isolation. A good Captain listens to their crew, recognizing the wisdom in each and every individual. In addition to informed decision-making, this collaborative process helps establish team trust and unity. Trust, is after all, a foundation for effective leadership.

Communication is crucial! :) Clear and conscious communication. The captain has to say, this is where we are trying to go, and here is how we should get there... and by the way these are the reasons for every maneuver. This transparency helps everyone singing from the same hymn sheet or plan of attack, thereby pulling in the same direction. But communication is not just about issuing instructions, it is also about listening. Creating an environment where the team members feel safe, to speak their mind, a captain who listens actively and empathetically.

An additional quality of a strong captain is adaptability. The sea is unpredictable and so is leadership journey. An example of this is how a captain should know when to move or adjust the sails and be flexible since the winds will always be changing. This adaptability means being not only reactive to change, but also being open to grown and learning. A captain that demonstrates a dedication to self-improvement is leading by one of the most influential examples possible.

No compromise on ethics and integrity The bolder the captain behaves, perhaps the more ready their commitment to what is right ought be. It acts as a moral compass that helps the team navigate complex, real life ethical situations — they use it to ensure that what actions they take adhere to high standards of integrity and respect. A captain who leads with honor gains the undying loyalty and respect of their crew.

Leadership is also about developing other peoples capacity. The leader pours themself into the growth of their team, for they know that the success of the journey relies upon having a crew strong enough to weather any storm. This means coaching, learning and recognition. The captain is increasing the capabilities of their team and a sense of ownership and pride in what they do.

There will be days where the captain steers through smooth waters, there will he days when the journey is tumultuous, but each day offers a fleeting chance to lead — representing a momentary responsibility as well as privilege. It requires immense courage, intelligence and a profound sense of responsibility for the lives of those they lead. A captain steers the path and influences the journey by way of what he/she does and doesn't do — arriving at them together symbiotically, paving the road to a common goal through resolute empathy.

Team Dynamics

They have been known to be the heartbeat of any successful organization,This infers that they help in changing circumstances as well. Thinking about it in my own experiences, I understood the complexity of interactions, communications and collaboration is what makes leadership effective. It goes beyond just getting the tasks done or hitting targets; it establishes a place where people are seen, heard and celebrated to be at their best.

I believe one of the best things about teams is that you get to work with people who think and solve problems differently than you. Every team member brings an individual perspective and ability to the project, so embracing that diversity can generate new ideas and ways of thinking. A leader also needs to realise the difference, not only in skills but how they relate to other people — just as on us — when leading them. Once they do, it becomes possible for a leader to construct a team that is all on the same page and feels like their input is being recognized.

And, communication is everything when it comes to team dynamics. Transparent, honest communication builds trust and respect among team members. Leaders must establish an environment where all can speak freely and be heard without ridicule or reprisal. They do this using active listening, constructive feedback and creating a safe space to speak up. The team members, who feel they are heard and understood, are more likely to get engaged in the common value of the team.

Although conflict by definition is confrontation, which leads to a clash or a battle among two; three or more parties (Konopaske, Ivancevich and Matteson, 2011), there are many advantages that can be brought about through conflict if it is well managed. Conflicts, disagreements and different voices are typical for any type of a group and may even benefit it as long as such process is carried out with respect to others in this group. The main function of any leader is to mediate conflict and, whenever possible, have the group arrive at a consensus where everyone feels heard. This solves the symptomatic problem but more importantly, when done right, which i will illustrate here and is an experience you have to try out for yourself because no matter how great my words might be they do not even come close to the thrill of going through the feeling that by doing simple mistakes you learn so much about this game.

Another essential element is trust among the members of a team. It is very easy to break, which takes a lot of time to build. You must have integrity, predictability and response-ability to be a leader that people will trust. And that is where the rubber meets the road, and it comes down to lip-service versus actions. When team members feel comfortable trusting their leader and vice versa, then the safe environment is created where everyone can take risks, be vulnerable to each other and support one another.

They weigh in with their fair share, but a lot rides on motivation and morale in your team dynamics. Acknowledging and rewarding achievements, no matter how big or small they are, can improve team morale and motivate synergy. It is about motivation, knowing what motivates everyone and seeing how you can put each players goal into specific KPIs. Another factor in employee motivation and engagement is the opportunity for professional growth and development.

This shows the value of good team dynamics and leadership — it is more than telling what to do, but also caring for whom to be. It is all about creating an environment where collaboration, trust and open communication blossoms. By identifying and capitalizingl on the strengths and diversity of each team member, a manager can create an antifragile high-performing team that will deliver impressive outcomes.

At the end of the day, leading is about people. Its about relationship building, creating community and most importantly, helping those around you be the very best versions of themselves possible. By paying attention to team dynamics, a leader helps everyone be a part of the conversation and helps each person have an opportunity to contribute — creating an environment in which everyone is important.

Motivating Teammates

It is actually the attempt to find from where motivation comes within you, and how your determination can be transferred so that you and your team are all motivated towards common goals. It is not the grand gestures but the little things that you do everyday to build trust and respect with your teammates. It is to acknowledge the strengths and possibilities each person can bring to the table, and it is creating a container where they feel liked or hated.

It is important to know what motivates all your team members. Recognition for some, new tasks to challenge others and past accomplishments of what they are personally capable of matter. It really pays to understand these subtleties as it can help you be a better inspiration. Effective networking requires active listening and a sincere interest in the dreams your new friend has for their career or life.

The one step that matters the most is establishing a culture of open communication. Engaged and motivated team members are created when they feel heard out. Get them speaking up and sharing their thoughts and not only are they more enabled, but they also start thinking like a player with skin in the game. It is a structured way of solving problems together and can help to unify the team at the same time.

Another important element is to set clear and reachable goals. Motivation decreases when people are unclear of their roles and do not know why they perform these tasks. Reducing bigger initiatives to smaller, more achievable tasks can help keep the momentum going and the sense of accomplishment along the way. Recognizing these little victories can make the employees feel good and strengthen a mindset.

Never underestimate recognition and appreciation of team effort. Public or private recognition makes people feel good and valued. Not only you should reward for achieved results but also to encourage hard work and dedication more important. Centering your praise is such a way that align with what speaks to each individual directly Turns these tokens of gratitude into something more significant.

A tremendous way to motivate your team is by leading by example. Start by showing commitment, honesty and passion in your work, that will then set a benchmark for others to keep up with. There is something very inspiring about seeing their leader be active and energetic. They will understand that you are not ruling up top but instead re in the same shit hole with them, putting your back into it and dealing talking to customers too.

Recognition and growth is a motivator as well. It sends a message to your team that you are taking meaningful steps in the interest of their longer-term professional development. And whether through training programs, mentorship or new responsibilities; injecting them with the desire of learning and honing their skills and knowledge all over again.

They need a positive work place. It allowed them to take risks and make mistakes, which is necessary for pushing the envelope. Developing a feedback culture that is supportive and not judgmental helps to build resilience and a growth mindset.

Motivating Co-Doxers with Reflective Leadership requires a mix of empathy and strategic thinking. It is to forge a home, one where everyone exists feeling understood, supported and valued as they mold their personal aspirations around the objectives of the team. It takes great time, effort, and the willingness to see others do well. These tenets will allow you to cultivate and engender your team, maximizing the output of each member, whilst also lifting them higher than they could alone.

Handling Wins and Losses

Leaders have to learn that it is the journey through peaks and valleys of success and failure that makes us good. It all depends on how we respond and what we learn from each event. Both outcomes are inescapable and necessary on the leadership journey. They build our character, strengthen our techniques and impart precious lessons in perseverance and humility.

Whether we success, it is simple as much time to feel the joy. So it is crucial to celebrate your wins: they help you remember what you have achieved and how much effort, time and team work has gone into getting this win. But it's important to have a little bit of the glass half full in those situations as well. One success should not be made to feel complacent or arrogant. It is not any of these things; rather, it should be a time to consider what has gone well, why it went well, and how we can take that good and make more out of it. Leaders also need to ensure that their teams are loved and rewarded for contributing more. This has made a motivational effort, but this will be your saving grace.

But then comes reality of facing losses which can be tiresome as well as humbling. Failures come with feelings of disappointment and doubt. Then again, these times provide as much — or even more — in lessons that are richer and longer lasting, compared to those we absorb from success. A reflective leader sees failures as stepping stones to higher performance. We analyze what went wrong, uncover the root cause of such failure and strive to identify how so we can manage it better next time. This helps to reduce the risk of repeating them in future and it also boosts the team problem solving skills. Fixing problems do not make it defect free but continuous retrospective meetings ensure that lessons learned are carried out to improve things better on those lines.

Dignified losses: Showing your poise and humility after a defeat is an admirable example to set. It shows that failures are not the end but part of continuing life to learn and grow. This creates a trust complete system when the leaders of that organization publicly talk about their failures and what they learned from it. It encourages team members to take some risks and innovate without the fear of failing.

Dealing with wins and losses is an emotional thing. Leaders must be mindful of the emotions, theirself and the others team members. One one side a win can bring without it a feeling of joy and accomplishment, on the other hand it brings pressure. A loss, on the other hand can be crushing but can also teach you to continue working faster and smarter. Great leaders know how to lead through that emotional reaction, both providing support and helping their team come down off of the mountain quickly yet effectively.

And how leaders play the win and loss gives us great insight into their character and values. People respect and trust consistency in behaviors; whether you win or lose. Leaders who are humble in victory and composed in defeat can build a loyal following of their team. They demonstrate that win, lose, or draw they are committed fully and completely dedicated to the mission and values of team.

Wins and losses, in that sense at least, are a part of the fabric and leadership weavings are layered with meaning. Successes and failures teach leaders how to be better ones. When leaders navigate these instances with thoughtfulness, equilibrium and emotional dexterity they not only lead their teams to success but also build a strong organizational culture that thrives through change and disruption.

Learning from Coaches

"Practice hard, work harder. The runs will follow" - Ramakant Achrekar (Cricket Coach, mentor to Sachin Tendulkar)

Coaching has always had a special status in the landscape of leadership development. The knowledge but also the complexity that textbooks and lectures cannot offer. Absolute wisdom from those who have walked the path before us can often shed light on a path forward. When I ponder some of my experiences, the most impactful lessons have frequently taken place experientially with a mentor where the lesson was less about the instruction and more about what we started to explain: raw leadership in its nature.

Perhaps the most important piece of learning to gain from coaches is their insight. A coach also personalizes their training for the individual, knowing that not everyone arrives with the same skills or readiness to embark upon a particular path. This customized outlook guarantees that the suggestions are not just timely, but also action oriented. I remember a mentor long ago telling me, Leadership is not about being the best in the room, it is about bringing out the best in others. This very simple sentence changed my paradigm, from looking out for number one to developing people and building a team.

Witness Leadership in Action - This is another thing that is absolutely key. There is often a coaching component that shows the principles in action, too. Seeing a coach manage difficult situations with poise and action serves as a model for aspiring leaders. Some of the best ways to learn is to watch others in action. Someone can read about conflict resolution strategies all day but seeing a seasoned leader in action as they diffuse a heated situation with their words and soft tone will yield far more lessons than any book can provide. Real life case-studies, soaking in the learnings much better than theoretical knowledge alone.

It also creates an environment of trust and vulnerability between coach and learner. It is a place we are safe to take chances and where we can confront our limitations and fears without criticism. This vulnerability is necessary to truly evolve. I recall one meeting in which I was reflecting on a difficult decision. He had not given me the answer but rather asked good questions that allowed me to find my own path. It also gave me an ability to make quick decisions, which helped build my confidence. Knowing that the answers were in myself made me feel stronger and showed me a lot about the independence needed of a leader.

Feedback also is important in the coaching dynamic. And constructive criticism, tactfully presented can be a perfect prod to making things better. A coach offers an outsider's perspective, at the same time shedding a light on some of our blind spots. I got feedback once that I often took over the dialogue, unintentionally crowding out input from everyone else. It was a light bulb moment that helped me take a more inclusive approach, which added more color to our team conversations and culture.

Finally, it gives the process time to work (something sadly lacking in some gyms). Leadership is an evolution of different paths that lead you to where you need to go next. It establishes ongoing support in the face of new challenges, and helps reinforce those important lessons over time. The lasting bond formed between mentor and apprentice serves as the foundation for developing meaningful leadership abilities.

"When you win, nothing hurts." - Joe Namath (American Football Coach/Player, New York Jets)

As I reflect on these experiences, it is clear to me that coaches not only teach, they motivate and push you beyond your comfort zone. This goes beyond professional development to affect how we think about and practice leadership. It is through their mentorship that we discover how to lead, and what it means to lead with purpose and truth.

V

Leading Cultural Events

Planning and Organization

In essence, some of the best leaders are ones who can paint a vision and plan every little detail to make that vision achievable. Most great things start with a blueprint, a plan that turns vague thoughts into action. It is not about just creating goals, it is regarding knowing the complex series of roads that take you there.

Planning effectively begins with a clear vision from the leader. The vision is a North Star that illuminates the way for every decision, every action. However, vision is not enough. To expose this, it needed to be broken down into manageable pieces systematically. It is here where setting SMART goals (Specific, Measurable, Achievable,

Relevant and Time-bound) is critical. These factors enable each goal to be specific and realistic, making it a Hell Yes or No walking paper for advancement.

The reasoning of resources, time and work aimed at achieving the best possible tasks matter. A well-kempt leader knows how to prioritize, delegate and manage time. It helps improve productivity and also incites team members to experience accountability and ownership.

To set good plans and get them in the right order would definitely need a great knowledge of the area in which someone operates. Those external opportunities and threats, like the internal strengths and weaknesses that will help drive your response. This SWOT analysis helps leaders anticipate threats and opportunities, allowing plans to be both pragmatic and anti-fragile.

Another key aspect is communication. As long as the plan is clearly articulated and makes sense, then everyone knows what they have to do for the overall team. This helps everyone get on the same page and work together to accomplish that result. Keep the team informed with provides regular updates and feedback loops in order to make any adjustments necessary.

In addition, flexibility is the cornerstone of good planning. Future leaders seldom stick to their initial plans —they are going to fail, and they must be ready for that. It takes a commitment to the highest vision but also the flexibility of being able to pivot. But it would not be wrong to say that this adaptability helps in diversifying the risks as well as catches certain secondary opportunities.

When it comes to organization, the machinery makes things much more running efficiently. These digital applications or tools such as project management software, calendars ease the progress checking, deadline managing and effort coordinating by providing a formal way to address things. When combined together these tools can turn tedious jobs into a simple set of processes.

When you think about planning and organization as fundamental leadership skills, it starts to make sense why they have such a huge impact on success. They turn visionary ideas into concrete results by making sure every action is intentional and in alignment with the bigger objective. A leader who is good at planning and organizing is not just a visionary but an excellent strategist, who knows exactly what zig or zag the journey is going to take.

The thing that differentiates a brilliant leader and an average leader is the capability to plot, plan things accordingly. It is the combination of both, their Vision and Structure on one hand for which connects to their Adaptability on the other are what make them be able to lead boldly and produce extraordinary outcomes. With prudence in planning and a systematic organization, leaders make their visions real inspiring their teams to scale new heights of success.

Creative Leadership

Leadership Unplugged: Less Routine, More Wild Ideas and Epic Brainstorms!

If anyone ever gave any thought of the question on what leadership is — essentially they would circle back to where creativity and command collide. Authenticity is not just a space of power, but a creative feast; the space where we undo the seam and emerge free — inspired, radicalized, on sight beyond that which everyone else can see. This unrepeatable confluence — where the pulsing heart of leadership heals not to the cadence of routine but to the spirit-beat of unlimited creative imagination — is what this chapter invites you into.

And, of course, creative leadership is not just a silo for those who are artistic or non-linear in their thinking. It is about creating an ecosystem where ideas can prosper, when team members feel encouraged to speak their minds without fear of backlash. It is successfully sowing a seed and then growing it beautifully.

A creative leader knows that success is not always a straight line. They understand the importance of taking detours and don't mind folding their plans up, they know that failures come to teach valuable lessons and see stumbling blocks as open doors. A leader like this is not afraid to take risk they are considered a necessary ingredient for it enables growth and creativity. They foster a culture where mistakes are not considered as failures but springboards to anything else more significant.

Creatively leading then translates into the art of facilitating and letting-go. It means creating boundaries and focus as well as freedom and permission. A creative leader is not a tyrant who tells his followers what to do — he/she is a facilitator and the person that helps unlock collective genius. They know that the best answers are frequently found in combining ideas, and incorporating different viewpoints.

Think about an inherent trait of being a creative leader-Let us take the example of Empathy. Empathy means connecting with your team as human beings, understanding their drivers, fears and aspirations. It is to provide a safe place where people are felt important enough, and their voice matters enough and enjoys hearing about their efforts. With emotional leadership as an example, loyalty and trust will be encouraged from the staff which creates a more vibrant team able to think creatively together.

Aside from creativity, leadership has to do with vision. Its a little over the line, thesedays ...to dream big — and to act on those big dreams even though they are scary as hell. A visionary leader is one who not only responds to the here and now but rather one who always anticipates what lies ahead, mapping a direction that others are motivated to travel.

This will mean a great deal of awareness on the part of this leader. Being able to put oneself in others' shoes. It entails self-awareness and the ability to change and be flexible. A typical customer would be afraid to ask for feedback but a creative leader never will. A creative leader knows that there is much more to learn, and they know how to refine without hesitation. They know that leadership is a journey not a destination, learning and growing every step of the way.

At the heart of creative leadership is a capacity to improve — i.e., both individual and development. Not just the challenges, but it is how you convert a thought into an actionable and executable idea and a group of people in an execution machine capable of doing events never done before. Its about leading with the mind, heart and soul motivating others to bring forth their best work that contributes to an even better world.

Engaging Participants

The trick isn't just getting them to watch the reels—it's making them star in 'em too!

In an art and science leadership development is a process of actively engaging participants. It is a complex role, it requires understanding of human psycheability to motivate and create this atmosphere where individuals are appreciated and motivated. Identifying intrinsic motivations of participants The first step in moving to engagement is recognizing what motivates participants.

Internal drivers are the forces within that spur action — whether it's a need for personal development, the call of duty, or the ability to create lasting change. A leader, by appealing to these natural inner drivers can cultivate a feeling of ownership and loyalty in its team members.

Open communication is the foundation of an engaged culture. Fostering candid conversation and respectful two-way communication is the foundation for trust. A complete commitment to the process is more likely when participants feel as though they are being listened to. This includes sharing information, as well as receiving feedback and adjusting accordingly.

Clear Expectations and Goals — This is another important factor to consider. People will stay focused and motivated when they know why they are doing it. The biggest reason for mapping out goals is to give people a destination — rather than driving aimlessly, they have a direction to go in that helps them to understand the larger mission and purposes of what they do. Setting goals both in the short and long-term so participants can experience progress and keep their momentum up.

Another key factor is to ensure that frequent feedback is given alongside these targets. Specific feedback is crucial for people to be able to understand where they excel in and where there are areas that they can improve on, information critical towards which developmental journey the individual might want to consider. Rather, one should give feedback that is supportive and non-judgemental, about specific behaviors and outcomes (rather than a person). It makes them feel valued and empowers them to be responsible for their own development.

The next crucial thing to do to engage the participants is community building. Personal connections among team members give people a sense of belonging and help to establish camaraderie. Team building through social events and interactions or simply encouraging informal connections can lead to a friendly work environment. If people feel a genuine connection to their peers, this is when you get the kind of collaboration and mutual support that nurtures what we call 'personal development'.

Powering the Participants: What is More Important This involves enabling them to tailor their actions and make decisions, through providing the required support-including resources. Believing in something greater than oneself encourages a sense of ownership and responsibility that drives you to be an active contributor to the team. It is the act of being hands-off enough to let kids work out how to do leadership, but hands on enough to create an environment that allows participants to flourish.

Another impactful way to keep participants engaged is by recognizing and celebrating accomplishments. Keeping those pipelines alive is just the part everyone sees... Publicly acknowledging both individual and collective wins reinforces positive behaviors, which in turn boosts morale. Above all, appreciation of any kind adds value. Keep in mind that simple acts of recognition also go a long way in making people feel good about their work. This is about the culture, to appreciate achievements and keep participants motivated to excel more.

At its core, participant engagement is about ensuring a space where individuals feel they are being heard, are inspired, and have power. It includes knowing what drives them internally, encouraging them, having clear objectives in place, communicating openly with them, giving feedback regularly and creating a community feeling among the team members, empowering them and recognizing their work. Identifying and then doubling down on these aspects are the first steps in creating an environment of engagement that will allow individuals and teams to blossom — and with it success.

Managing Resources

With regards to leadership, resource management is crucial for a good leader. Time, money and human resources are limited. These assets need to be connected in order for a leader to be able use them properly and then take their team or the project toward achieving its goals. It is a whole strategic thinking process that goes beyond allocation; it is about foresight, flexibility and continuous improvement.

When one thinks about resource management at its core, it first requires a comprehensive understanding of the resources in play and where they relate to team goals. Which is needed in a leader as it combines the analytical and gut sense. Analytical as in how many resources, their limitations and how to use them. Able to recognize what is likely hidden within the team as well as within alternative ways of working.

Time, one of his most precious resources for a leader. Time is not replenishable like other materialistic resources. Great leaders are always doing things that tie to their strategy which make it easier to spend every second available, moving closer to that bigger vision. Which in this case means making hard choices about where to focus and what to outsource. Delegation is not a task-passing mechanism; it is a trust and growth-building activity. A leader is more bashful freeing up own time and enables with parts a construction containing smash naked and development.

While these are less abstract, financial resources require the same level of thoughtful analysis and strategic planning. Budgets are not only about monitoring what has been spent but strategic planning for the future and allocating adequate resources in order to thrive. A true leader is always alert and working on various vectors to make sure that spending is optimized without a loss of quality. But it requires a delicate balance between caution and boldness, knowing when to hold back and when to invest in the levers to propel.

Your team is also your human capital — the most changeable resource that there is and, as a leader managing this asset, you have to be both a coach and instigator. Knowing more about where a team member is coming from helps in allocating tasks and makes better work. A culture that makes individuals feel seen, heard and inspired to participate at their best. That includes clear communication, celebrating wins, and providing feedback for continual improvement. So, it is about creating a culture that not only allows constant improvement but encourages it as well.

Cultural norms and the structure of resources - Adaptability as a critical factor to managing resources A leader needs to be able to see that the landscape within which his / her team operates might change and they should be willing to pivot strategies accordingly. There are also the preparedness to adapt according to new information, and readiness to try different strategies knowing you can always change course based on feedback loops. From them, I have learnt that flexibility does not mean without a compass, but with the willingness to change the route as long as it is for arriving at the goal!

Improvement in every area of resource management — this is a common thread. A leader should always keep measuring the success of their strategies and ready to have small updates. This means keeping your self abreast of the latest tools and methods, taking team feedback seriously and a fundamental investment in improving yourself. Progress is not an end, but it is a journey, and one that requires persistence and making the necessary effort.

Allocating resources is only a part of effective resource management. Indeed, it is a story of vision, strategy and the power to inspire, change and evolve. It is there in the reflection leaders have, gathering strength to be able to lead teams towards their own success and making sure that every resource would go a long way.

Reflecting on Experiences

Reflection is a keystone of leadership. And in the pause, you can Explore and Learn about all of the different scenarios playing out. Not to cry over spilled milk, nor even bask in the self-congratulation but it's a complementary side-order about what you have learnt and will never do again.

Reflection of experience is a very important piece, and the most crucial thing towards this regard, is to possess an evenly viewpoint. Leadership requires people to make decisions quickly on-time or under pressure.

Seeing The Forest Through The Trees At times: How to see the forest through those trees, which often just look like a bad horror movie where your face is an inch from the screen. The only difference between leaders and followers is that the real leaders know when to "pause" their work, go google maps street view or zoom out (aka take a selfie from 30'000 feet! — joke!) Take a breather and from that vantage point, actually see what the hell has been happening to you; identify those hidden lessons amidst the fiasco at hand so you can...you guessed it.... crush your next go around!

If you are not honest with your reflection, it will not work. It involves a certain degree of uncomfortable self-exploration and taking responsibility for the world they have created. That would provide a different kind of truth, the sort necessary for progress. This human element makes it a more meaningful exercise to think for thinking's sake, without it thought can seem quite trivial. It makes you more reflective and forces yourself to face some really tough questions: How should I have handled this differently? What was the impact my behavior had on others? What were the unintended consequences of my behavior decisions? Leaders that take the time to ask these questions receive feedback on their actions and its aftermath.

Like the Mirror, feedback from others is also essential to reflection. It is, of course, good to know yourself but you are blind to your faults and even you cannot be totally honest with yourself thanks to bias. We can attach some kind of colleagues, mentees and team members to transform further standpoints directly into this sophisticated reflectivity. Configured feedback focuses on that which we did not think of or new aspects of old beliefs. It promotes teamwork, allows the team to free up themselves and propels the ball into rolling towards improvement.

Reflective theory in writing - The role written reflections can play The benefit of this is that Writing down thoughts, and observations makes things organized in a cohesive way and also makes it more trackable over the period. A white paper on reflective practice for leaders A journal-based approach for reflection — the leader keeps a leadership journal to which he or she comes back to time and again, noticing how thoughts and insights unfold over time. This sort of documentation could never be expected to remain up-to-date, but it will serve as a handy reminder for when you need to retrieve things that are not immediately apparent.

This way, if we have nourished the muscle of reflection enough, it will no longer be a too-occasional occurrence but something rather more common in our day to day life. Adding the above questions into your leadership weekly or monthly cadence of conversations slowly brings this practice back into a more natural way of leading for leaders. Using this in your life will look like organizing times of reflection (for example, at the end of a project or before an important event). Reviewing regularly will help to develop reflective thinking as a habit in your practice for personal and professional growth.

This reflection from the individual level is necessary, and when you can, some reflection as a team could also be useful. The debrief and group discussion process may bring up shared emotions, AND (if the level is appropriate) this can surface some collective learning points. This shared responsibility not only develops inner business relationships but also overall improves the learning process.

Leaders who adopt reflection as a pivotal leadership tenet demonstrate their own growth and set an example for others — it's normal to take pause, step back for perspective, and recalibrate.

Eventually, it all comes down to the expectations we make and even changing our ideologies. For leaders, it helps them to feel more in control over the complexities, and basing decisions off of it.

VI

Know when to Shut up!

Active Listening

Spoiler Alert! - It's not replying to someone while you are scrolling reels.

Listening is one of those tasks that we assume get handled automatically, the same as going through and refreshing Instagram, zoning out in random video calls. Listening for real, like listening in a way that takes it all in as if you're an absorbent pad — you suck up the vibes and the words. And It's not just sitting there and nodding; it's about being fully engaged, like you're binging on your favorite show, but instead of that this time, you're streaming someone else thoughts.

I like to refer to that as "active listening". And honestly, it's a little leadership secret. You have to be there — not just listening, but in the room with them; picking up the body language and underlying cues like you're decoding their character. When somebody imports, it is rarely just about fetching the words; you have to decrypt the entire emotional mixtape that hides within.

The initial step in becoming great at active listening is to be there. Have the decency to put aside your phone and look them in the eye! This involves tuning out any distractions like mobile phones or other activities and giving the speaker full attention. To present your physical presence, that is too coarse and rude; but the same with mental and emotional presence. When you show up completely, it shows the speaker they matter, and that can revolutionize how you engage.

Active listening includes attention and non-verbal aids. More eye contact, nod more, and use facial expressions to show you are interested in what is being said. Inflection cues signal to the speaker that you are listening and make them feel more comfortable opening up.

Repeating back what you have heard is another important aspect. This is generally performed by simply paraphrasing and summarizing the speaker. So let's say something like, "It sounds like you're worried about the project due on Monday. Is that correct?" It lets the speaker know that you are listening, and gives them a chance to explain or elaborate.

This will even broaden the conversational horizon with guidelines through open-end questions. Those questions encourage more detailed answers and prove a willingness to learn what the other party has sacrosanct. So instead of asking, "You happy with how the project is going?" In that same conversation, you might ask, "What do you feel about the momentum driving the project right now? This way tends to elicit a more fleshed-out answer.

The cornerstone of active listening is to listen empathetically. This includes understanding not only the words being spoken but also emotions behind them. By listening empathetically, you affirm the speakers feelings and demonstrate that you are interested in their experiences. This could be something as simple as, "It seems like you're disappointed with this situation. I can totally understand why that would be difficult.

Being patient is key in active listening. Is it exactly what untold measures must be implemented to herd the wolf that you lent an ear to, let him speak (not interrupt) all out? Doing so can be especially tough in high-pressure industries where time is of the essence, but it is important to establish a relationship of trust and comprehension. This is a sign you are more concerned with your perspective that theirs.

Do remember that active listening is a skill, and one which develops over time with practice. This will likely feel foreign and you may struggle the first few times — especially if you are used to multi-tasking or preparing your response while someone else is talking. Practice active listening to make it as natural for you as breathing — your leadership and even your relationships will improve, not to mention the general quality of communication.

If you are in a leadership position, then active listening is that much more powerful as communication and relationships are crucial in any chain. This shows respect and generates cooperation, which could result in better decision-making.

Tip : For continuity use these 2 golden words - "Really?" or "Strange!" and see what the magic unfolds :-)

Speaking in front of a Crowd

In my humble experience, my golden rule has always been to remember the "ABC and XYZ of public speaking" ABC - Always be Cheerful and XYZ - eXamine Your Zipper.

The experience of speaking in front of an audience, be they a small group of fellow professionals or a large auditorium full of interested listeners, is exhilarating and intimidating. Playing to the crowd is not only about what one says, but also getting the message across at a higher level in order to galvanize them and leave an impact. Based on my own experiences, the road to mastery is paved with self-awareness, candor and growth!

One of the first principle, I learnt was to be authentic. And when the speaker is genuine, the audience can feel that as well. Authenticity means being real and sharing your raw, full self — the good and the bad stuff. That means speaking from the heart, not just reading out a script. Once, I was speaking about how to rise against adversity. Instead of a simple read-through of my notes, I told a story from deep down in the trenches about something that went wrong for me. The room went quiet and it was evident the weight of my words. After the talk, people came up to me not to applaud my eloquence but to thank me for my candor and boldness. It was an important lesson in tricking us to reach the deeper, more resonant level that authenticity will at every time surpass perfection.

Preparation is another very important part of public speaking. Sure, you still have to be spontaneous at times, but keeping your act relatively well prepared allows you the freedom to rise to any occasion. And that does not mean learning each word by heart, but instead everything you say comes directly from understanding what you are conversing about; which comes from researching and tracking the sector in a dialogue in this sort of way that it feel extra natural. Once I had only a week to prepare for a conference talk. While the theme was common territory for me, I also realized that I needed to go beyond surface level and offer something more valuable. I had been doing endless amount of research, note making, and practicing for hours. I was at ease when that day finally arrived. This preparation kept me more engaged with my audience, able to answer questions and even change up parts of my speech accommodatively.

Another crucial aspect is the engagement. You cannot just talk to your audience; you have to engage them in a dialogue. You can accomplish this by making eye contact, asking questions, or just adding interactivity. I remember running a workshop where I invited everyone to share their beliefs and experiences. The room felt alive with the change from listening in a passive way to listening and engaging. The conversation was richer because people were involved and the session had a depth to it I could not have achieved.

Effective Communications Flexibility in public speaking is also necessary. Even the best-laid plans do not always account for unforeseen hurdles. A misbehaving robot, an audience that was paying no attention whatsoever or just plain old nerves. Above everything else, you have to be flexible and calm. One time the projector broke during a presentation, so I was left without slides. Rather than panic, I saw it as a chance to be more upfront with the audience. I moved around the room, looked at my audience and used tone with expression when I made a major point. I got a lot of good feedback, and hey, a number of people said they felt more attached without any slides (any barriers) between them and the talks.

When I think back on these, it's easy to remember that speaking in public is not simple, a tool built over time and with much training. This is not just about information sledding, it is about bonding and embarking a change to leave something that lasts. Whether you are giving a briefing to some number of your peers, or broadcasting to the wider community through the press or social media, these principles can deliver great benefit. Every time you have an opportunity to share your voice, it is a chance for you to get better, learn from an audience and become more of the leader we need in this country.

Non-Verbal Communication

Nonverbal Communication: When Your Face Says 'I'm Listening' But Your Body's Like 'I'd Rather Be Napping!

Nonverbal communication is a powerful form of leadership that largely goes unacknowledged. Our movements, facial expressions, body language and even the way we look at someone from the corner of our eyes all reveal our feelings. This non-verbal communication either supports or contradicts what we speak and determines whether those who follow are left feeling inspired or bewildered.

Some apply the concept to having to stand before your team speaking with confidence, optimism and enthusiasm about a demanding project. And your words affirm: "We can do this!".. but your body is scrunched, your arms are folded so defensively, and you are eyes dancing everywhere in the room When there is a disconnect between what you say and how you say it, your team knows and that lack of congruence can sabotage your credibility faster than shit through a goose. It's not only what you say, but it's how you say it and carry yourself as well.

Eye contact... one of a leader's most powerful weapons. They can show sincerity, confidence and attentiveness. Maintaining eye contact demonstrates that you are fully present while eloquently speaking. It creates rapport in a way that words cannot. But, there is a difference between making well-contacting eye contact and just staring, which can make people uncomfortable. The golden mean is to be sufficiently engaged without being intrusive.

Expressive gestures are important in non-verbal language as well. Open body language, like extending your arms or revealing your palms, signals that you are being open and honest. Collaborative: They solicit collaboration and indicate an open door. Conversely, closed gestures such as folding your arms or clenching fists provide barriers and the opportunity for negative emotions like defenselessness/aggression to be expressed. Watching your movements will assist in helping you look confident and open.

Another important factor is posture. Even the simple act of standing up straight with your shoulders back can make you feel a bit more confident. It is a physical display of confidence that can effect your mental state and thus, effect how you interact with others. On the other hand, if you are slumped or hunched over, you appear tentative and less confident. Be attentive to your posture as it plays a big role in looking like the leader you want to be.

Our facial expressions show a glimpse of our emotions. Cut a real smile — It SHINES and projects warmth while making you approachable (psst, people will be more likely to connect with you this way). On the other hand, even good words said with furrowed brow or frown indicates disapproval or frustration. The ability to be aware of your facial expressions and make sure they match what you are saying can improve your leadership skills.

However, non-verbal communication is more than just about interpersonal interactions. When you are in a meeting or speaking in public your body language will dictate the direction of the room. Whatever the walking, physical stances and manner are, it should demand attention and lend authority. It is about building skills where your mere presence can motivate confidence and respect.

Avoiding mixed signals is just 1 of many aspects of verbal communications. We will still lead, but we will begin to mobilize every component of human expression into how we lead more effectively. You make your words match with the way you carry yourself, but in doing so, aligning what is heard with how it felt — Through this congruence of spoken language and body language. You are nonverbal in leadership, acting trumping language time and again, which can make the silent ordeal of body language one of your strongest assets.

Persuasive Techniques

Persuasion: The Leadership Power-Up That Makes Everyone Want to Join Your Party!

Having the power of persuasion is akin to starting at a mountain peak, or using an infinite cheat code that opens every door on your path to reclaiming leadership over your life. It is not only about making people dance to your tune as if you were the leader of a TikTok or Instagram challenge, but also about instilling belief and introducing a suitable flavour to which everyone can relate. Persuasion is the amazing marriage of a bit of logic and a bit of feels, with lashings of some psychological pizzazz.

Ultimately, people resonate with leaders who they have respect for. Credibility? No silver lining here... that is your leadership street cred. Be good and they will come [to the reddit, we hope!]. Your Words Hit Different When You Lead With Integrity Trust is yours Wi-Fi signal for all the rest of your persuasion powers to work. Without it, you're buffering.

Its all about knowing your audience. Everyone is motivated by different things; fears and ambition drive each one of us. A leader who knows his shit listens, and watches to hear what is important to those he wants to get on board. Empathy and a more personal approach ensure the message is tailored, relevant, and resonates with the receiver It is not about using emotions as a lever, but establishing deeper connections.

And persuasion is BIG on logic and reason. If you can formulate arguments based on evidence and present them in a clear, well-structured manner, even the most skeptical minds can be made to think again. But, it is equally as important to mix facts with storytelling. Narratives: As part of their evolutionary history, human beings are heavily pre-disposed to narratives and this why they can help in simplfying complex concepts and make them more relatable as well as memorable. Leveraging your message with data helps other people remember what you want to say.

Interestingly, one of the most powerful mechanisms in play to tackle this challenge is emotional. Facts hit the Brain, feelings reach the Heart A great leader knows just what the best emotion need to be evoked at any time. That might be a sense of urgency or hope, even a call-to-action. Through this leader is able to enkindle others with the fire in their own hearts and motivates them to act passionately.

The greater the coalition of support one can build, the easier it is to influence. Propagation — it gives instant credibility and reach to any message when others are seen championing your cause. Build trust and community When people feel that they belong to something bigger than themselves, they find meaning and purpose and will then invest their energy and resources;

Never underestimate the significance of paying it forward. You know how that old saying goes, what you give is what you get or something like that and it sort of works on the principle of if you show some love and spread some good vibes, people will want to do the same for you, kind of like the universes' "you scratch my back I'll scratch yours" situation.

The magic ingredient What all this boils down to is reciprocity; whether you are sharing your knowledge, hyping up someone´s work or retreating their hustle! It is basically the cheap hack for social relationships and being good at winning people over.

The timing and context are huge factors too. Timing also plays a huge role in the way you present your ideas. A timely message is crucial in ushering a paradigm shift and expanding consciousness. On the other hand, an argument delivered at the wrong time can fall flat even if it is extremely compelling.

Another form of persuasion is non-verbal. One way the 3Cs transparency strategy can be achieved through good body language, eye contact, and tone of voice that makes us appear more confident, sincere & authoritative. These subtle nuances can make your message stronger and more persuasive. When you are conscious of the way that none verbal takes place is when your communication will resound.

This is not about manipulation or coercion. It is leading others toward an objective with honesty and dignity. By using those somewhat manipulative techniques, a leader can create true buy-in and create a team-spirit. Becoming a leader is not something you just learn how to do and then fine tune over time, this process of becoming develops continuously, it evolves and the skill of persuasion can make all the difference in an effective level of leadership.

Feedback and Improvement

Feedback isn't a roast, it's a guide. If you take it right, you'll be glowing up in no time. Feedback is one of the most powerful tools it provides in terms of growth and that ever-evolving cycle. And in my experience — feedback is so much more than the exchange of information: it's a courageous, and humble dance.

I remember my first leadership role, where I was instructed to lead the team of four who were all different races. I was more or less inspired by proving myself and so I did not pay much attention to the subtle signals my team was signaling. I only started to learn the skill of LISTENING after one of my trusted colleagues took me aside, and gave me some brutally honest feedback. This was a defining moment for me as this is when I first understood that you do not have to demonstrate authority in leadership but create an environment in which every voice can be heard.

Feedback is a mirror, showing not only our qualities but likewise where we lack. It is uncomfortable, but it is in this discomfort that real growth takes place. One time, a team failed to complete a project together. Now, instead of just point fingers, we all gathered and dissected what went wrong. Simply put, the conversation was vital to sharing insights that enabled us to navigate around those same pitfalls in the future. This highlighted the need for a learning environment where feedback is not perceived as criticism but as one of the ways to power growth.

Part of the responsibility of a leader is not just to receive feedback but also provide it in ways that are constructive. Through the years I have discovered that how feedback is delivered can make all the difference. It is a fine line that must ride between being honest and empathetic. I once managed somebody who was underperforming. Instead of dwelling on the flaws, I celebrated their strengths and recommended tangible actions they could take to get better. This helped increase their confidence in themselves and also had a visible upgrade in the quality of work.

It will constantly be about progressing, and that requires accepting self-reflection, and adapting. I spend a lot of time looking back, not to beat myself up about the past but to learn where could I have done better. And now, it really is how I lead. Reminding me that perfection is a lie, and the pursuit of goodness is forever.

For organization-wide growth, developing a feedback and continuous improvement based culture is important. This culture starts from the top down and it's leaders who create that tone. Leaders go first by asking for feedback and showing that they are committed to evolving, empower their teams to do the same. This creates a ripple effect, in which the pursuit of perfection lands in the organizational DNA.

Looking back on these experiences, it has become apparent to me that the feedback and self-improvement game is one of personal growth just as much as professional improvement. It forces us to face what we believe are our boundaries, and then it dares us to push against them. They teach us that leadership is a journey, not a destination. A route that is both hard and promising...inviting vulnerability yet leading to a level of personal leadership ability beyond what I could have hoped for from myself.

VII

Get that Time Management on Point

Prioritizing Tasks

Time is like your phone battery—use it wisely before it runs out!

I remember when I first started in a leadership role, of the thousand things mulling around in my head that demanded my focus and attention. All of them appeared as crucial as others, all to be a nightmare if not managed. It was a constant spiral and I always felt like I was responding more than influencing. This haphazard process was not only a malpractice; it would be unsustainable. It soon became obvious that to be an effective leader, I would need a new approach ... task prioritization.

The most important lesson in prioritization is to realize that not all tasks are equal. The level of urgency and importance in tasks is hierarchical by nature, and recognising this hierarchy is key. Feeling clueless, I found my way to the Eisenhower Matrix where tasks are arranged into four quadrants of urgent & important, not urgent but important, urgent but not important and neither urgent nor important. This simple paradigm shift kind of changed my life. This simple plotting of tasks in this matrix allowed me to easily see what actually demanded my attentions and what should be handed-off or postponed.

We are naturally inclined to jump ahead and try to knock out everything we consider urgent or important, but in many cases this sense of urgency puts us into the vicious cycle of firefighting. However, tasks which are important like but not urgent can contribute in longterm. Even worse, these are the strategy assignments that ensure a vision is established and growth materializes but is frequently drowned out by day-to-day needs. Purposefully carving out time for these responsibilities keeps the foundation of leadership both solid and forward-looking.

But that said, perhaps the most important part of setting tasks in order is ensuring they are aligned with the bigger picture. Task, however small, should be programmatically supporting the overall objectives of the team or organization. This alignment ensures manpower does not go to waste on activities that dont move the needle. Busywork can be disguised as productivity, and that was a lesson I learned the hard way. Through always asking "does this task takes us closer to our goals?" I was able to trim away the excess and get back to what was important.

It also means being flexible and adaptable. The leadership landscape will continue to evolve, and what is hot today will not be yesterday. Task management rigidity may cause missed breaks, overlooked crises You need a happy medium to be structured but able to change as you go. Such dynamic prioritization demands constant retrospection to re-evaluate whether the emphasis on what changes tasks.

An effective prioritization is largely dependent on communication. You have to communicate it to the rest of your team, so they will be able to see for themselves what needs to go in front of what. Preference clarity guides us in the order of priorities, managing expectations and insures that everybody is paddling one way. Team meetings and open discussions around priorities helped to achieve a collective sense of mission & responsibility.

Finally, there is the personal level of importance where some jobs are more critical than others. The demands of leadership are equally as demanding, if not more so, in your personal life as they are on the job. These never-ending to-do lists can suck you into a wormhole that will never let you go out and take care of yourself which in turn leads to burnout. Incorporating personal priorities into the task list is a well-rounded way of leadership where life and work go hand in hand.

Ultimately, it comes down to being more thoughtful about your choices around given tasks. It is about cutting through the noise and knowing where to spend your time, money and effort that give you the best chance of growing. It is something that comes along with experience and should be inline with may pave the way for effectual leadership. It still stands as a fundamental of my approach to leadership and how I navigate through the dimensions of entrepreneurship.

Tip : Focus on the 80/20 rule in all areas - Find out which are the 20% of inputs that lead to 80% of output. Double down on them to progress much faster.

Avoiding Procrastination

Procrastination is like scrolling Instagram. Fun in the moment, but suddenly, 3 hours are gone and you're still in the same spot.

The competitor on the battlefield who competes for effective leadership is procrastination. But in too many cases, it is merely a cleverly packaged stealth raider of time and potential. Through my own experiences, I remember thinking that procrastination was a small luxury at the time while in hindsight I wonder just how much of an effect those delays had on my end goal.

One vivid memory stands out. At the start of my professional life, I had a work where planning was everything. Instead of jumping in and DOING the work, I started getting DISTRACTED and then began lying to myself that everything was going to be OK. With days passing into weeks, the deadline was looming and now a source of stress. This cut down on the quality of work that I did, and as a result I lost out on showing just what I was capable of doing. And that was a wake-up call, the blunt reminder of what I had lost by procrastinating.

Why we procrastinate is best understood first to be overcome. Most of us fail, or are trying to be as perfect possible. It really had me thinking, and I noticed the underlying reason for my hesitation was doubt. I had been waiting for the right time, the plan to be perfect, but perfection is not real. Irrespective of the associated volatility, leadership demands action

One of the most far as I have recently decided that breaking these things down into smaller pieces has been a life changer. It was easier to focus and make progress when I had those clear, attainable goals. It seems like this way of doing things made those tasks less scary and they were able to celebrate each time another thing was ticked off the list, rather than waiting for recognition after inching over the line with all other main activities as well. This is a theme I pitch to lots of budding leaders — and it comes back down to the little regular things which build momentum.

Prioritizing my time, by working on the most important and urgent task first was a fantastic technique that i have found invaluable. That is when the Eisenhower Matrix became a simple and effective tool. Things like catagorizing tasks meant I worried about what was actually important, not lets get busy doing nothing tasks. This change in mindset was freeing and helped me to focus my time and energy elsewhere.

Accountability too was important. When I shared my goals with a friend or mentor, that gave me some accountability. The above also ensured that I successfully practiced my language learning skills daily, and sometimes an outside perspective is best. It is something I advocate for my teams to do with each other, helping build a self-sustaining culture of trust and co-ownership.

Contemplating the significance of self-discipline has made me realize how routines play a huge part in it. Creating a routine for myself with something very similar to my Pomodoro timer, I built up some self-discipline and a lot of the temptation to put things off till tomorrow disappeared. These small things, like listing the top one thing I needed to do each day, or literally marking out three hours on my calendar as "work" instead of waiting until motivation strikes, helped incredibly a lot.

Recognizing that procrastination is a reality that even the most experienced leaders face is necessary because it helps you learn to tackle this challenge head on. Different leaders equally understand and feel it, but what differentiate is, perception and action to correct it. With an awareness and utilisation of tactics, procrastination can be turned around to act as a mechanism for growth.

Because procrastination is more than a personal struggle; it affects the whole team. Another way to put it is that taking swift action and making decisions quickly as a leader sets an example for others who you might inspire, too. This establishes a culture of accountability and focus on the objectives resulting in more spirited and efficient pursuit of these goals.

In hindsight, I realize that there is no real cure for procrastination. It takes diligence, introspection and a willingness to be better. We commit, or rather, we open up our potential and choose the path of purposefulness — clearly.

Tip : Activate the "2 minute rule" - If a task takes less then 2 minutes to complete, do it immediately.

Effective Scheduling

You wouldn't binge-watch a show without knowing how many episodes there are, so why go through life without managing your time?

The most important non-renewable resource you have as a leader is time, and all-too-often; your time can be wasted on tasks that are out of alignment with the goals of the company. As I think about it, even in my own life at times, it feels as if we are being tugged in several different directions leaving little space for what is really important. This lesson served as a very powerful reminder about the impact our schedules can have on how we lead — and live.

Prioritizing is where it all starts. If you do not have a clear idea of what matters, it is very easy to get crushed under the tidal wave of things that seem important all trying to grab your focus. Pause and reflect on wider long term goals, what you need to do in order to get there. If you align your daily activities with these goals, then your time is being spent where it matters. Personal Alignment: and not just from a professional career goals perspective, but also from personal life one too as your balanced life have an important impact on how effectively you can lead others.

Once you're clear on what your priorities need to be, the next step is in allocating time to allow for that. It takes a strong focus on scheduling to accomplish this. I vividly remember a time in which my calendar as packed with meetings, one right after the other; leaving no room for deep work or strategic planning. It was only when I started to schedule different blocks of time for different activities that I saw a dramatic increase in my productivity as well as focus on mental. Without going into too much detail, this just means dedicating large chunks of time to a specific tasks and not bouncing from one task to another ensuring that you get the focus time each task deserves.

In addition, it is necessary to add buffer times. This is very true since life happens and more often than not, some unexpected task or emergency comes up just when you thought you were settled. If you strategically add buffer times to your scheduled appointments and tasks, it creates a margin that gives you the flexibility to get through something unexpected without throwing off your whole day. This not only lowers the expectation but also helps you be more agile and mindful in the face of unexpected hurdles.

Another crucial part of good scheduling is delegation. Go through the tasks that take up your time, but might not need you to do them. Passing these off to a competent team member not only gives you time back but empower others — which leads into building trust, along with fostering some collaboration. Well that is a positive feedback loop: they win and we win, it boosts productivity in general and morale.

Modern technology can be an incredible asset for creating effective scheduling. Dropbox Dropbox For saving files like receipts, payments, plugins etc we use drop box along with Google Drive Slack Slack It is a collaboration tool that helps teams to work together effectively G Suite Gooogle G Suite Use for emails, documents, spreadsheets Tasks & Reminders (Inbuilt) Getting things done on specific time and date is must Or there are apps Number of tools are available in the market which can help managing the task and sending reminders and tracking progress. But the manner in which you deploy these tools is vital as they should contribute towards your time management rather than serving as distractions. For example, establishing individual moments to critique email can lessen the regular interruptions that will break your frame of mind.

Now that I look back at where have been, it reminds me how important frequent reviews of what am doing with my days really is. What was good one month is outdated now. Continuous improvement occurs when you regularly test your schedule and make adjustments based on what is and is not working. It is an iterative and organic process that requires continuous refinement in order to ensure that you are always perfectly harmonized with your goals and responsibilities.

This also goes to show that effective scheduling isn't about filling every minute with a task, it is all about having a planned and balanced way of managing your time. So you lead better and live bigger, by putting first things first, budgeting time, building in margin, delegating wherever possible & using tech as leverage to constantly refresh your calendar. This habit not only increases your overall productivity, but also gives you a sense of accomplishment and daily purpose.

Balancing Responsibilities

Balancing responsibilities is like mixing a playlist. You need a little bit of everything to keep it fresh and vibin.

Juggling the demands of modern life Life often feels like a jugging act, with multiple hat, and responsibilities vying for our time. We all have busy lives, whether it be professional obligations or personal responsibilities, the endless list of things that need done can leave us utterly exhausted. The most effective and impactful leaders, however, are those that inherently merge these aspects of leaderships with their core values — something I must actively remind myself to do regularly.

During my early career, I was seeking to establish myself in the business and realize as much revenue as possible, so instead of passing leads for smaller loans off to a lower-producing service partner, I wanted every loan on which I could pay them commissions. I did in fact grow up believing that saying "yes" to everything was the way to make it. But it just ended up making me tired and taking me away from things that really mattered. Only when I started to take a step back and evaluate my agenda...did I learn why balancing was, in fact, so valuable.

One of the most important lessons I learnt was to use boundaries. I realized I had to be selfish with my time in order to make things work. So I had to practice saying No: no to tasks that did not serve my main interests. It also demanded that I learn to pass off duties and rely on others to carry some of my weight. The benefit of this was to enable me to concentrate on those areas in which I was needed and offered the most value.

Then there's the key component of balancing duties: Time management. So, I broke down my day into time blocks allocated for certain activities and that kept me in a pretty consistent state of flow when working. This helped me manage my energy a lot better and reduce the fuck load of multitasking that I had been doing previously. When I aligned what tasks were actually important with the urgency that I felt from my perception of those items, suddenly it was much easier to make simple decisions about where to spend time.

Think of responsibilities like your phone notifications—manage them, or they'll take over your life.

Self-Care: This last point is more important than any other, the importance of maintaining that balance. We all get busy and taking care of ourselves often goes by the wayside. This helped me realise that I needed `me time` — or activities that re-energised and nourished my body, in order to maintain the enthusiasm for what I DID want. It may have been breaking a sweat early the morning, stilling your soul during meditation time or engaging in quality relationship building with someone, Sounds that gave enough space and distance from leadership roles.

Communication also helps a lot to balance the responsibilities. I also found that the more open and honest conversations I had with my coworkers, family, and friends, the better we were able to communicate expectations between us so we avoid potential disappointments. After I declared my requirements and boundaries, our relationship was kinder: we were inclined to reciprocal precautions and empathy. This worked to take some of the pressure off my shoulders and also encouraged accountability for each person in their specific role.

Looking back on these experiences, I have slowly started to view balance not as something we get but as energy which flows. It calls for continual reassessment and reiteration based on the prevailing circumstances. Sometimes, we have certain things in our responsibilities that demand more attention at the time and it is okay. The trick is to stay pliable and open, consistent with our mission to realigning our actions with our higher selves in perpetuity.

The humanity side of it all is the one thing that allows us to struggle and still show ourselves mercy in the light of it. Settling for nothing less than perfection is futile, and it is completely fine to be a little easy on yourself. By creating balance, we gain the capacity to role model more effectively and clearly with a greater sense of purpose, presence, and pragmatism. This in turn, allows us to empower and uplift others intentionally ensuring a positive ripple effect.

Using Technology Wisely

Catch that Tip at the end of this chapter, it's Free !

Tech feels a bit like the future and a little hard to get right in our modern world. Its not just about getting cool new shit for peeps in charge, but utilizing these tools to make their team perform better and achieve whatever goals they have. Contemplating this balance makes me realise that the true heart of wise technology usage is to ask yourself why and to mean it.

Just ponder over the types of tools that you can now see in a few clicks, from communication to data engineering and other AI tools available. They each bill themselves as optimizing efficiencies and insight, but without a strategy they quickly become distractions. Before leaders can determine how to adjust and fix the conditions, they need to understand exactly what challenges their teams are facing. This realisation becomes the underpinning for the respectful integration of technology. Do the coolest tools first, but make sure they fit the concept AS WELL as being groovy and very now.

And a leader should not just select the right technology but foster an environment where team members can use these tools in the most effective way possible. At the same time, training and continual learning become essential. Through implementation of robust training programs, leaders can ensure their team is not only capable but confident that the tool has much more to offer than what they are using. Inspiring a spirit of invention and innovation often results in groundbreaking inventions and effectiveness.

In addition, we should see technology as an augmentation of human potential and not a substitute for it. Despite all advancements in automation and AI, there are certain things where human touch is irreplaceable— empathy, creativity, critical thinking. The challenge for leaders is finding a balance to free up their team's time to focus on these higher-order tasks, while also using technology effectively. This not only improves productivity, it makes people happy and helps them grow personally.

Another extremely important aspect where the use of technology is a boon as well as a bane simultaneously, is communication. Teams collaborating/chit-chatting via instant messaging apps, meeting on video conference calls is not something new now days. That said, the accessibility afforded by digital communication means that things can easily cross into overload and cause work-life separation to blur. Anyone in a position of leadership must establish strict rules for how people should refer to the machines so that technology can be used effectively, rather than misused. This is about creating a culture that leverages technology to enable high-quality and focused communication without distracting or overwhelming the team.

Another level where the beneficial technology is Data-driven decision-making. Leaders can now make rapid, informed decisions using real-time data and analytics. However, the amount of data can be overwhelming. Leaders need to cultivate an expert sense of what metrics are important and how to interpret them correctly. Intuition & Data — Data may not always be readily available to make the "correct" decision so having a healthy mix of analytical skills and intuition is required to ensure that decisions are informed by data but also context local.

This is perhaps the filtering down of information on cybersecurity, a side of integrated technology that doesn't get as much attention as it should. Today in the era of data breaches and hacks, it is a must for any leader to secure all their employees/clients data. These include investing in hard security and also promoting a culture of vigilance and responsibility. Frequent training on cybersecurity best practices can be especially crucial in protecting the company's digital property.

After all it comes down to the leader and their adaptability, foresight and more. Pivot: The space is moving as fast-paced, tools and trends come in and out of fashion — to future your tool means that you will have the time to pivot it early and reassess the utility. Leaders require a relentless pursuit of knowledge to inspire constant examination on how to utilize technology as an extension of vision and goals.

When you really sit down and ponder on these principles, it is somewhat obvious that technology can be used as just another tool to assist adjacent the lifestyle of a ruler. Thinkful must be approached with thoughtfulness and commitment to learning — and at its heart, it is about the human moments technology cannot replace.

Tip - Your social media history is omnipresent, don't post something you are not gonna be proud about in 5 years from now.

VIII

Start giving a Damn

Emotional IQ

Emotional intelligence is like your Wi-Fi signal—if it's weak, good luck connecting with anyone!

Our actions, decisions, and ways of interacting are shaped by the Invisible currents called emotions. They were the silent forces that rule how we see, and how we are seen in the world. These subtle yet powerful forces are, in my opinion, critical to understanding within the domain of Leadership.

This got me thinking about my own past leadership experiences and how emotions had so often been a driver in steering the course. There were moments of joy and triumph, when nothing else in the world mattered but us — & other times of struggle, doubt, frustration. This realization opened my eyes that these emotional undercurrents were as essential to leadership, if not more so than any management theory around.

Self-awareness is one of the things you need to start doing for being able to understand emotions. It includes recognizing not only our own emotional reactions, but also the reasons why we react. I have vivid recollections of one project that seemed to be a daily exercise in failure. Originally both of these things caused me to growl in irritation and push, action now! Based on time and exposure to such challenges, I realized my trigger points and developed an attitude of moving past patterns rather than throwing patterns back in the mix exposed to me.

Understanding Who we Are – Empathy, Rage It is understanding the experience of other people, viewing life through their eyes and empathizing with them. I remember one team member telling me about work-life balance. I was able to give that suppport and create a stronger team environmenta by listening without judgement or prejudice but with the emapthy of coming from a place where I had certainly experienced something similar.

EQ (emotional intelligence) is a combination of self-awareness, self-regulation, motivation, empathy and social skills. This mix is what allows leaders to traverse emotional terrains of confusion among team members. I remember in the past how stressful it became for the team when faced with a tight deadline. Letting those feelings be known and speaking about them could promote a sense of support that would enable each individual to operate at their peak despite the stressors.

It also means being aware of how your emotional state manifests itself onto other people. It is a well-known fact that emotional states are contagious, and leaders lead the way. I mean, at one point I remained calm and composed when life unexpectedly threw me a curveball. Their calm and composed nature encouraged all of us to work on this solution with a clear mind, as well as unitedly.

Further, the ability to make sense of emotions is a fluid, continuous tuned process. This is an ongoing process of reflection and adaptation. Every interaction, every decision and response creates an opportunity to find that understanding. In my experience, the realisation that you can be radically wrong sometimes and that your view of yourself and others is a perception helps to start building this Flash Judgement Muscle — it comes with regular self-reflection, feedbacks, and learning from both success & failure.

In the vast tapestry of life which is totally leadership, emotions are what bonds you to humanity. They impact on the trust culture, collaboration and resilience across teams. When leaders learn how to use emotions in a positive, affirming manner, they can inspire and influence their teams in ways that make each member feel important, heard and willing to offer their skills most effectively.

Looking back on these reflections, it is clear that attending to emotions does not amount to simply controlling sentiment but cherishing the entirety of human life. It is more about understanding the intensity of a leaders motions and using that understanding to create empathic, resilient and resourceful leadership.

Empathy in Leadership

You know you've got empathy when you can feel your friend's pain over a breakup and still make them laugh about it with a solid meme.

When one stops to contemplate the very core of leading, it is difficult to avoid focusing on the importance of empathy. It is essential to leadership, but it more than that it actually changes the power dynamic between a leader and his or her team. With empathy, people can connect on a deeper level and build trust and respect. Empathy helps leaders really connect with employees as people, making more thoughtful and kind decisions.

In the modern business world, it becomes easy to err on the side of seeking results over relationships. Rather, the true beacon of loyalty and commitment comes from leaders who are able to understand what makes their team members tick — their experiences, struggles, and what they imagine for themselves. It makes you feel like you belong, and nudges and encourages everyone in the team to work better.

Think about the change a passionately listening leader could provide. This leader isn't listening to words, rather the emotions and desires behind them. In their willingness to hear and validate the feelings of others, they create a culture of safety that helps team members feel seen and connected. Application of this practice not only boosts morale but it also promotes team communication and collaboration, which are ingredients vital to the success of a team.

Conflict resolution also requires empathy. Disagreements are natural in any team. A leader who empathises more effectively negotiates better in such situations. Through grasping the root concerns and feelings of those concerned, an empathetic leader can help reach a solution where all involved have their perspective accounted for. Such an approach solves not only the immediate problems, but also unites a team and increases its endurance.

In addition, If you think empathy is just about feeling sorry for someone, then you've clearly never tried to comfort a friend while they're scrolling through their ex's Instagram.

It also requires having the chests to understand the broader context of your team members. This should be about understanding external constraints, your circumstances in life and the universe you operate on. A leader that expresses such a high level of empathy generally tends to be effective in giving what the team members want and require to achieve better results. They can predict possible trouble spots and reduce the chances of them occurring, which in turn makes the workplace less hostile to work productive.

Thinking back over the years, I remember one leader whose vulnerability directly impacted my career. One of my managers worked closely with me to go through a tough project to see where I was under the most stress and facing difficulties. Instead of demanding results is supported me with encouragement which made me get over those blockages but also increased my respect and loyalty to them. This experience demonstrated how powerful and effective an empathetic leadership can be in driving motivation and performance.

Empathy is not something some people are just born with and others are not. It is something that can be mastered over time. However, leaders can practice empathy by stepping up and showing up with presence, active listening and curiosity around what others are going through. It takes time, thought and empathy to put yourself in someone else's position and respond with kindness.

Empathy is an overseer to the leadership process, if leaders can not connect with their team on a human level, they are unable to succeed in their mission. It turns transactional relationships into real connections, encouraging all of us to notice each other and appreciate one another. Empathy is what enables leaders to motivate their people not just to deliver organisational objectives, but also through far more profound personal development and fulfillment.

Tip : Practice a random act of kindness everyday. It could be as simple as giving someone a compliment. This wont just boost the mood of the person, but will also make you feel good!

Building Relationships

Building relationships is like playing Tetris; you've got to find the right pieces to fit together, and sometimes you end up with a mess!

In my experience, I have found that leadership is not just about pushing a team towards a target; it is all about relatability and the person. At the heart of effective leadership lies relationships. That is the conduit; where trust, teamwork and respect pass through it. They are not built in a day — they require effort to listen, support and empower all of those people we care about.

Without doubt, one of the biggest lessons I have learned is how vital it is to be able to listen carefully. All i am doing is listening to someone, but not listening in the way that my ears pick up sound waves — Instead, I am hearing through their words and understanding their emotions, motivations, concerns. This kind of listening is done with patience and empathy. It means letting go of what I want and pouring my heart into someone else.

Listening I believe has enabled me to develop my relationships more that anything else with my team. They feel their place is valued, they feel listened to which creates loyalty and commitment.

Showing heartfelt appreciation is another essential component of relationship building. Even just saying thanks, or a word of encouragement can make someone else feel worthy. A team member once went the extra mile to get a project done, I never forgot it. And instead of just saying how hard my team were working in a meeting, I sat down and wrote every one of them a nice thank you note for doing that extra little bit more. The reaction was direct and forceful. This made the team member feel appreciated and inspired to keep up their hard work. This has shown me that little acts of gratitude can vastly enhance relationships.

Honesty is also important. It has to be by people you know that they can trust their leader. In times of tough choices and struggles, I learned that being honest about the situation and communicating transparently with my team creates trust. It shows: I care about them and I respect their ability to handle the truth, whatever it may be, yet we can still overcome together. Transparency creates a culture of openness that allows people to contribute their suggestions and opinions, which in turn comes up with ideas for more innovative and better solutions.

Another key pillar is support. Leaders who are always ready to offer help and guidance Simply, this is being a person that people can reach out to. I remind my team on a regular basis about their welfare as well. I have an obvious respect for their lives outside of work, showing them I genuinely care about them as people, not just employees. It truly solidifies the relationship between us and helps maintain an environment where we support and inspire one another.

Relationship-building also includes celebrating success together and failing forward. When we hit a milestone, I make sure that everyone takes a pause and celebrates the combined effort. That creates collective success and keeps the focus on the one team mentality. On the other hand, when it all falls apart, I bring together a meeting and try to open up discussions on where we fell short and how we are able to go better. This instills a culture of continual learning, and support for each other.

At the end of the day, relationships are that you show up, that you are real and that you be helpful too. It is identifying and appreciating the unique ingredients that every individual brings to the table in order to craft a setting where everyone comes together as one body with one spirit working towards building something great! By building on these relationships, we can influence and lead much more effectively, forging a strong and motivated team. These experiences remind me that at the core of leadership is not being afraid to connect with others in a direct and impactful manner.

Managing Stress

Stress is just a fancy way of saying 'I'm not sure how to handle my life right now!

If you have a problem, and you know you can do something about it, why worry?

If you have a problem, and you know you can't do a damn about it, what's the point in worrying?

Being a leader naturally comes with stress. Pressures of decision-making, weight of responsibility and non-stop need for results together make a thought-storm collides with hard reality, causing some serious anxiety and tension. Looking back on my life, and particularly at health-related events, I realize that stress would always be there; it was not about getting rid of it so much as managing, minimizing and working with.

At one point or another in my leadership trek the pressure has been overwhelmingly sad. I had sleepless nights, continuous worry, and the paralyzing fear of falling down became my daily companion. But these tough times also taught me another priceless lesson on fortitude and self-reflexiveness. The first thing you must do to handle stress is accept that its there and acknowledge what it does to both your mind and body.

There was one period where I felt like the director of my department, whose workload could conceivably outweigh multiple day shifts a day. Deadlines were coming fast and I was tasked to lead my team whatever it takes. In times like this, is a simple but very powerful tool that mindfulness and self-reflection. In those days I would intentionally devote some time or take out of my schedule to simply deep breathe and center myself. A quiet space, a reminder that even among the chaos there is always room for peace.

Alosso, Health Science Major tells us what she believes is the importance of boundaries when it comes to helping manage stress, Thanks. Leaders often feel compelled to have ongoing, overly detailed involvement. But that kind of thinking can make you burn out and less useful. So for me, it was learning to fight against my natural tendency to want to do everything myself and allow my team to help. By doing so, I not only took burden off my chest but also empower my team members where we shared the responsibility as a team effort.

Our response to stress is very much connected to our health. I discovered that consistent exercise beyond something as simple as a brisk walk brought clarity to my mind and courage to my emotions. When we are so caught up fulfilling our responsibilities as leaders, it is easy to forget the need to take care of oneself physically. It reminds again that to care of ourselves is not a privilege, but a requirement.

Another important stress management tool is connecting with others. Confiding to trusted colleagues and mentors about my struggles and vulnerabilities gave me new perspectives and much-needed support. These discussions would often remind me that I wasn't alone in what I was fighting for, and therefore serving as a form of comfort and appeal.

It is also necessary to acknowledge the mental aspect of stress management. But seeing those challenges as an opportunity for growth, instead of a mountain too high to shimmy up, offers us a perspective shift that can help looses our grip around ourselves. I worked on reframing my thoughts to what I could control, and letting go of...well the same thing! This shift in mindset changed everything for me as I was no longer executing these tasks with a heavy heart and finally had a sense of purpose.

Stress is part of the leadership journey and a skill that develops over time. But with self-awareness, assertiveness through boundary setting, the encouragement to make health a priority and permission to ask for help as well as a shift in perspective around leadership we can graciously and resiliently hold onto the powerful roles that intrinsically bring such tremendous pressure. Every experience, good and bad, makes us a better person and lets us lead more effectively.

Remembering those experiences now, I see that stress is hard but it can be an amazing teacher as well. The biggest failures in our life often result from the toughest challenges — forcing us to face off against difficult truths and awkward realities, seek breakthroughs, and in that process to grow as leaders. The journey of creation cannot be thwarted by resistance or hesitation, but it will stall when not greeted with an open heart.

Self-Regulation

Practicing self-regulation? More like practicing the ancient art of 'not scrolling for five more hours.

Self regulation: It is that thing you can not avoid which makes exceptional leaders, well exceptional and simply good ones passable. It's the ability and practice of regulating our emotions, thoughts, and behaviors in different situations. One who requires nothing from those around them, a nearly self-regulating leader can determine their way through the murky waters of leadership with clear water and unwavering grace, always moving in concert with their values and what is best for their team.

The first and maybe most important piece of the puzzle is self-awareness. One multi-triggered dimension that is helpful to understand involves emotional triggers and responses. That means looking into one's own soul and acknowledging one's own flaws, confronting one's biases. Leaders need to be aware of their emotional state, and know when they are calm or agitated. It gives you the ability to make a decision about how you handle your emotions — rather than becoming a victim of them — In one case, a leader can simply identify the stress in their lives and therefore take a mental break to think about and consider approaching the issue with a sound mind.

The next level of maturity after self-awareness is emotional regulation. It essentially refers to how one manages and modifies his emotional reactions. Such techniques as mindfulness, meditation, and deep-breathing are incredibly useful. These are helpful tools to keep you at ease, as well as maintain your focus when under stress. A more advanced one (in terms of separation) is what psychologists dub cognitive reappraisal, which consists in reinterpreting a situation so as to influence its emotional reaction. Leaders who see adversity as a process of development not a inimical force can keep an optimistic and constructive attitude.

There are different sets of techniques for warming up, and greater focus on behavioral regulation. It is about managing one's behavior — and reactions to stimuli — over time, given what a person really desires to accomplish. And that usually means postponing immediate satisfaction as well as answering to the urge. This might mean not making an instant decision as leaders and waiting for more data, pause, or strategic consideration. That also means having defined goals that you can achieve and the discipline to keep going despite all of the distractions and setbacks along the way.

Self-regulation also includes how one regulates their behavior and emotionality in the context of interactions with others. Leaders should be emotionally intelligent like auras as they can get what their people are emoting and act accordingly. Here arises the most important role of Empathy - Having to sense and face the feelings of other humans will strengthen trust and lead towards a more supporting, collaborational environment that a Leader can generate. This boosts motivation and increases the overall productivity.

Self-regulation is not a trait but a state, and it can be taught as process. Leaders are constantly learning and getting feedback, then working to build upon their experiences. The practice of learning + adaptation reinforces their capacity to self-regulate over time.

The path of self-regulation is highly individual and, however, determines how well you are able to lead. This means leading yourself to lead others well. There are other ways leaders navigate the complexity of leadership, by cultivating self-awareness, emotional regulation and behavioral discipline that help them move through the work with grace and resilience. A skill when developed, can impact the leader as well as the very team and organization they lead.

IX

Networking and Building Solid Links

Importance of Networking

Consider networking as your personal Avengers assemble team, except you are not there to save the world but rather survive adulting. Think about it as a game of percentages, but the more awesometastic people you know, the higher your chances in beating those curveballs!

I am looking back at when I first entered the world on Leadership and wanted to share with you how I downplayed the power of connections. I came to realize a strong network can only be forged by treading the path of problems and in my case, tough challenges. These were not "just business contacts", but people with whom I shared insights, talked about experiences, and moved my journey along.

Thinking back to those days, I can clearly recall one of my first conferences where I felt completely out of the loop. I stood in a corner, watching people who seemed to float seamlessly from one conversation to the next. I was afraid and it was too hard for me to go talk to random strangers about important things. However, it was in that discomfort that I actually decided to step up. I walked up to a small cluster of people, introduced myself and listened more than I talked. When we departed that night, I walked out with more than a stack of business cards; I had laid the foundation for lifelong relationships and friendships.

Remember- networking is far more than a transaction. It's about creating real relationships of mutual respect and things in common. To listen, and in turn share your own knowledge and encourage them too. What I have learned so far from the journey is that it is always the best connections formed when there are pure exchange of thoughts and learning. Lots of growth I owe to these connections.

There was one example that I will never forget. I was given a life or death decision which also had an effect on my team. I reached out to a mentor I met five years ago at the same conference for advice on what I should do next. She was incredibly insightful, not only because she knew what I had been through but also because she just got my flavor of crazy. She shared something that I had not thought of, and it was this external view that assisted me to handle the trial with no problem.

This extends far beyond just solving problems. Everyone has an attitude of learning and becoming more. My network has exposed me to different viewpoints and new thoughts that have influenced my leadership style. Learning new trends, industry best practices, and the latest technologies. These insights have allowed me to be one step ahead and make smart decisions for my company.

Networking is also reciprocal. I have benefited greatly from my connections, but I also was able to give back. Getting to mentor others, sharing my experiences and supporting them has been the most rewarding experience. This has only furthered my opinion that leadership isn't about leading others but rather encouraging them to follow their passions.

Effectively, networking is also a key part of leadership. This is not just about growing your network, but growing more deeply in relationship. It also focuses on fostering a support group, friends who can exchange freely about knowledge and experiences. Being open to ideas and perspectives, and being prepared to give them in the future. Some of the scenarios in which I was placed during my networking experiences allowed me to understand that leadership is not for one man all — but it is a road walked together. The ties we bind as we go, are the threads stitching together our leadership iguana.

Building a Network

In hindsight, many of them were not a product of a single individual but arose from the kinds of connections that form by chance due to either the right people being in the right place at the right time, or enough good fortune. The connections we form and sustain are the sinews of substantial management, weaving a web of backing, intelligence, and openings that can shove us on our path.

Not realizing the power of networking in my early years. The way I saw it, hard work and talent were what you should be rewarded for. But over time, it became clear to me that the most effective leaders also had large networks of people they could rely upon. They had created their circles of people—a variety of various groups the could learn from, that would push against what they thought and empathize in times of need.

It is about developing long-term relationships with like-minded people who possess the same principals, love for life and dreams. May it be always giving as much as you take — or even more. The effect is establishing a strong foundation of trust and reciprocity based on transparency — one that stands the test of time dormant free relation honoring from initiating any exchange as long as you approach networking with authentic intent to help others.

I went to a conference when I was only starting out in my career — and very out of place among people who were already pretty close to being grey-haired folks. That's where I met a mentor who would help mold me into the leader that I am today. It started like any other conversation but eventually became a place of rest and encouragement. This mentor who not only gave me ideas but also introduced me to various other people from different fronts in the field that I had no idea they even existed.

Networking is all about being genuine. People instinctively know when you are real or when you are trying to leverage them. Trust = Authenticity, and Trust is the foundation in each relationship that really exists. By being genuine when practicing networking, you facilitate a safe-space for meaningful connections.

Diversity is a crucial part of networking. It Is Easy to Stay in Your Bubble Unless you are open to meeting new people and hearing different ways of thinking, it is easy to stay surrounded by like minded individuals who look like you. Find those that have different experiences, background, and abilities. Such diversity will enhance your knowledge of the world and bring you a well-rounded leadership style.

And do not disregard the power of INFORMAL NETWORKS as well. Good relationships aren't always built in formal facilitated settings, they often happen informally over coffee or drinks. The casual settings also offer people in their more genuine light and this can create deeper bonds.

Consistency is also crucial. The firm caution that building a network is not something we can do once and forget. Stay in regular touch with your network — give them a helping hand and be woven into the fabric of their lives. All this ongoing effort will ensure that your network remains healthy and alive, there for you when you need it.

Looking back on my journey, I realize that the biggest advantage I ever had was the one single connection that would lead me to another. Some of the people I have met have offered mentor-ship, guidance, support opportunities that my own efforts would not even come close. Leading is not a solo act; it requires us and the connections that we make.

As you continue on your journey as a leader, remember your network is indeed a great deal more generous and wise than you even know. Be real, be inclusive and work on it. This will in turn create a web of community that not only bolsters your success, but also adds to the essence of who you are as a person.

Maintaining Relationships

In the great woven fabric of leadership, those ties which bind us to others are perhaps as important as the vision that drives us. The spirit of leadership lies not only in guiding but also in fostering the links that ensure and enhance a team leading to its bigger version. I look back on my own life, and no wonder, I find that the very foundation of leading is staying connected to relationships — those tender tendons of empathy, trust, and shared regard.

Therefore, the first step to understand team relationship dynamics is self-awareness. You must know your strengths and weaknesses, but also how these impact your interactions with other people. The way a leader and their team connect with each other can subtly affect, influenced by the emotions between them and definitely of the biases that come in play. Cultivating a habit of self-reflection — instead, allows a leader to enter relationships from a place of wanting to understand the lived experience and aspirations of their team member.

There is no relationship without communication. Transparent and frank communication contributes to trust, so that team members can see themselves understood and appreciated. In other words, it is about hearing more than about speaking. The simple act of when a leader practices listening those they lead, it is validating their experience and perspective which helps to build the base for trust. Leaders accomplish this when they walk the talk and are genuine, which all contribute to making them credible.

In the same vein, you must acknowledge and reinforce their individuality as well. Each and every person has their own special mix of skills, experiences and perspective to offer. A Leader in a way also has to acknowledge these differences and appreciate them, as that will create an inclusive and respectful workforce. This includes acknowledging the hard work of team members and encouraging their skill development. Acknowledging their interests and providing possibilities for advancement helps respect their well-being and future. Insuring loyalty and dedication act as the by-products in this scenario.

Conflict is unavoidable in every relationship and where the manner a frontrunner dispenses with it may break or make the connection's bonds of a group. We must learn to view conflicts as something to be resolved rather than someone to be blamed. It has to be done patiently, open-mindedly and with the desire for a genuine common ground. An effective leader will help diffuse issues and promote a safe workspace by addressing these assumptions immediately to prevent future misunderstanding.

Furthermore, a leader does much more than just work stuff. By displaying real compassion for the personal affairs of team members, you can build strong bonds. Small acts of kindness, like regularly asking whether they are okay and commending their accomplishments can establish a feeling of involvement and fellowship. It is in these seemingly minor gestures that lasting effects are usually created.

As I recollect what stands at the core of leadership, it becomes clear that the power of a leader is directly proportional to the power of their relationships.

Connection — this is where the leader cultivates, sparks and leads their team to a singular vision. Skills in preserving and fostering relationships are not fixed but rather an active work of learning and development. It is our responsibility as leaders to always form connections, respect and value everyone.

Tip - Remember their birthdays, anniversaries and make sure you call and wish not a mere text message or meme.

Leveraging Social Media

Social Media: The Only Place Where You Can Be Both Famous and Awkward at the Same Time!

Social media has become a powerful weapon in the arsenal of any modern leader. It is capable of connecting, inspiring and mobilizing like nothing else. Personally, I have witnessed how platforms such as Twitter, LinkedIn and Instagram can revolutionise not only businesses but individual leadership styles.

Authenticity is an integral aspect of social media use. In an age when everything is curated to perfection, authentic, heart-felt communication shines brighter than ever. It is important that as a leader we show our wins and losses, and share with the world who you truly are. Your vision, your triumphs and struggles create an even stronger connection in the hearts of others. And trust is the currency of any fulfilling relationship whether that be on-line or off.

Engagement is another key factor. Social media is a two-way street—it requires engagement. Interacting: By responding to comments, weighing in on discussions and recognizing others input you will transform your brand from just another account into a lively, engaging community. This engagement will not only help promote your message but also demonstrate that you value and acknowledge the perspectives of others, a quality needed in all leaders.

Content is, of course, king. But quantity is not the only thing that counts; quality is equally important. Did you find an interesting article, thought-provoking quote, or have a personal tidbit that provides value? You could push this out and let people know your brand knows what they are talking about. But, just as necessary is listening. Because it is a special side through which you can read the minds of your audience, their issues and hopes — social media. A leaders must be aware of these in order to shape their leadership accordingly.

Another powerful aid is the storytelling visually. People are visual beings first and foremost — pictures or videos communicate messages more effectively than words ever could. From showing a sneak peak behind the curtain of your work, to displaying special team victories and sharing in personal moments of reflection — visuals add layers to your story and make it easier for viewers to relate.

The timing and the consistency of being posted is important too. We already know leads take a few months to convert into closed customers, so consistent and frequent content keeps you relevant and top-of-mind for your ideal customer profile. But that's a tight rope to walk; too much can cloy and seem cutesy, too little and you might sound like you don't care. The right formula for that just takes a bit time and effort to uncover i.e. the habits & likes of your target audience.

And on the other hand, social media offers us unprecedented opportunities for being inspired, learning from others, and just allowing ourselves to grow. You can stay updated by following the industry leaders, attending webinars and joining groups. So that you can continue to learn how to lead.— It keeps your mind enriched with knowledge, makes you a better leader.

But he is also happy that the digital world of cyber space does not come without its downsides. Because of the immediacy and reach of social media, these type of blunders can have huge implications. There is honestly nothing wrong even doing it considering the potential long term implications. It genuinely Matters What You Post? Certainly, thoughtfulness and discretion are key.

In my experience, when I look back and reflect on my journey the most amazing thing that came out of social media was forming real legitimate human relationships. Each of these connections have made leading in this work not only more joyful, but also much more meaningful —I couldn't have predicted them any better if I'd planned for them. How else do you receive impact from your leadership, access to executive support or ease of closing business?

Stay Flexible and Open to Opportunities As the world of social media is constantly changing, so must the methods we adopt. This you can do, which will bring out its absolute power to not just change the way you lead but also affect those whom you lead.

Networking Events

Going to a room where you do not know any body can be frightening, but those are the rooms where some of the most transformative bonds are built. And do not be deceived by the misnomer "networking" event, these fora are more than just a place to distribute business cards; they are the jars in which relationships ferment, strategies coalesce and destinies crystallize.

I remember walking up to my first networking and feeling like I was back in high school. The entire room hummed with conversation, laughter and the sound of glasses ABOUT to click together. For the first time, I noticed that networking events are actually a lot to do with listening as they are answering. Listening is an underappreciated skill while being one of the most important ways to connect. When you listen, it's a demonstration of respect and a sign to the other person that you care about them because relationship is established on understanding one another.

Moving through the crowd, I realized authenticity is at the heart of making a true connection. Being authentic is something people can feel and they really react to it. What really ended up working for me was shedding the script and my fancy title, and instead opening up about what I love, what brings joy to my life, and where I could use help. Authenticity removes barriers and create a place for real conversation to take place.

A followup lesson I garnered was you have to give before you can get. Networking is often seen by many as a transactional process, and while transactions are important to any growing career, the most fulfilling of these exchanges comes from the best place: genuine generosity. The whole give before you get mentality, the helping hand, and knowledge sharing, being supportive type of kindness opens doors no other self-serving was way can. You create a wider and deeper network when you see networking as an opportunity to give.

Being prepared is another critical one. Seeing where you ultimately want to go with your event helps keep the direction and intent behind it in focus. If your goal is to find a mentor, get feedback on a project, or learn about potential collaborations with someone, knowing this ahead of time can help you maximize opportunities as they come up. Prep work also means having a short, interesting response to the question of who you are. A memorable elevator pitch may leave a mark, but it should also be versatile enough to benefit from conversational context.

Network effects are also pervaded by continuous learning. Sidebar : Everyone you meet knows something you don't.

When you interact with people, who are not the same as you, it broadens your own perspective and you learn new things that are alien to you. These incidents also reinforce the fact that learning never ends and everyone that you come across in life has something to offer.

I have come to see that networking events are not only an opportunity for professional networking, but community-building. A tribe that has your back, pushes you to be better and lights a fire in your soul. It is a world-in-miniature, where many-stranded paths meet and new courses are taken. They are the ones who teach us that leadership is not a solo act, but a shared journey whose richness comes from the relationships we build and maintain both as a reminder and an inspiration.

And in those busy rooms with endless opportunities, I discovered this: networking is about so much more than opportunity. The stories you share with each other, the comprehension and supportive feedback form the real power networking holds. These events remind us that leadership means not just leading but also being part of a community of leaders working together, forging their destinies in the name of growth and success.

X

Problem-Solving and Decision-Making

Identifying Problems

Like Spotting the One Relatable Relative at Every Family Function!

So, when it comes to leadership, spotting is an art as well as a science. A talent that separates the best leaders from the rest. Problems are not always acute or what you think; they can hide in layers, mundane happenings, or plain old routine. The first key to being great at this skill is adopting a curious and mindful mindset. You need to see beyond what is presented, challenge the norm and dig a little deeper to understand what might really be going on in your team or circle.

Establishing an open dialogue is one of the best ways to screen for problems. By allowing team members to voice concerns and offer observations, they transform into a rich mine of information. A culture of transparency is one that means even the smaller things are spoken about when something happens. Leaders need to actively listen to these voices and understand that what may sound small could very well be a manifestation of a larger and more far-reaching problem.

Another important weapon in a leader's armory is observation. This way helps the leaders to understand what is going on in their team and probably find some small red flags as earlier you learn the problem better chances are that it can be solved. That might mean a dip in work output, changes in morale, or ongoing team member conflicts. Though not always definite, these signals can alert us when things are not well. And it is the watchful leader, bearing an ever-conscious gaze, that is truly effective.

On the other hand, problem identification goes hand-in-hand with data-driven decision making. Use Metrics and Analytics. To help leaders understand how well their team is doing and where they can improve, they should use metrics and analytics. They identify areas where things are not going the way they envisioned by analyzing trends and patterns. Following an empirical methodology helps identify problems based on evidence rather than purely relying on gut feeling.

Leaders also need to reflect on their own behavior. They need to be honest with how they dealt with their choices and actions. At the heart of other problems that exist in a team or an organization, one could directly attribute it to leadership practices. Recognizing the source of the problems at hand, a Leader can work to correct them. They need humility and a mindset that always seek to improve.

It can be downright prudent to retain external perspectives as well. Leaders should not hesitate to reach out and talk through things with a wise sage, friend or other expert. They provide new perspectives and can catch issues that internal eyes may have missed. External perspectives will be able to challenge your assumptions and possibly provide other ways to look at the situation.

In the end, it is an always-evolving process of identifying what is wrong. It requires you to react in advance on every level. These insights combine open dialogue, careful observation, data analyses, self-reflection and external consultancy to help you have a holistic view of the problem at hand. This way of working helps to detect real problems more accurately and at the same time trains heads in their efficient resolution.

When it comes to the whole concept of leadership, being able to diagnose is fundamental. Everything hinges on this first act of thought. Leaders who master this aspect are more likely to understand how to manage the complexity of their role and help their teams thrive and succeed.

Tip - 5 Whys? Take a problem statement and keep asking 'why' 5 times to get to the root-cause.

Generating Solutions

When I reflect on the process of coming up with solutions it is clear that this phase also represents a pivotal point for leading. It is the place where vision confronts with reality and ideas should be shaped into an action plan. The ability to solve problems is not only an expertise to practice but a form of art that demand creativity, critical thinking and collaboration.

First, in this process, is to drill deep into the problem. It is not enough to have a surface understanding without the details and reasons behind it. This nuanced view is usually developed through active listening and sharing empathetically from all parts of the stakeholders. Its asking the right questions and a real interest in the answers. Without them answered, this is all built on a bed of quicksand.

And then comes the most crucial part — Brainstorm. It is a space where different ideas can be generated and none of these could be immediately shut down due to the fear of judgment or practicality. A place where creativity is encouraged and out-of-the-box ideas could be brought to the table. This is where leaders are key; to transition, they have to ensure all voices are heard and empowered. It is in this mix of ideas that many innovative solutions are born.

But, the creation of ideas is not actually an end. Unfortunately, this is what the ideas need to be: sieved through and polished. That all comes with critical thinking. The process for evaluating a new idea must be to assess the potential impact; ease of implementation and also how aligned that particular idea is with the goals. This is the phase when one needs to strike an equilibrium between optimism and realism, meaning to be open but also keeping the practical side into consideration.

Another pillar in the creation of a solution is collaboration. Which is building a team where everyone has different viewpoints and is good at their skill. A common goal leads to trust, open communication and true collaboration.

Leaders need to manage group dynamics and promote a culture of creativity with collective problem-solving.

Not only that, the process to create solutions is iterative. This is a process of ideation, feedback, and iteration. The first one is rarely the finest solution. Great leaders know the importance of rethinking and then reformulating their plans with fresh data and views. Not only does this improve the quality of the solutions, it also helps to develop resilience and adaptability within your team.

We also tend to forget that it takes enormous Emotional Intelligence in order to build up on emotions and generate solutions. Leaders have to be aware of the emotional heat in their team, registering stress, irritation or indifference. Dealing with these emotional undercurrents can make a huge difference in how effectively solutions are generated. This means providing a safe space for team members so that they can feel important and inspired to give their best.

The last puzzle is the power of articulating the selected solution in an effective way. This includes more than simply showing the answer but explaining why it makes sense. No matter the approach or modality, leaders need to be able to articulate the problem clearly and guide stakeholders through the solution side of the process as well as help them understand implications on several other levels. Creating transparency and breaking down is deceptively simple, but it rallies everyone around effort and delivers everyone into the implementation in alignment.

And basically the solution generation process is multi-faceted; it requires analytical skills, creative ability, emotional intelligence and collaboration. It's the testimony of just how complex and rich good leadership is; making the way from problem to solution as important, if not more so than, the destination.

Evaluating Options

Reflective leadership entails more than just decision-making, its making the appropriate decisions to begin with and this requires consideration of ones options.

Leaders approach choices with a careful consideration of the various scenarios, using their intuitive sense together with analytical thinking. However, the first step involves obtaining all relevant information and dissecting the pros and cons of each option. It's not just a 'you write the pros and cons in the boxes' but also an appreciation of what both those paths could lead to.

Take note of why a decision is being made. What appears to be good today may not seem that great tomorrow. The world of business and leadership has become increasingly dynamic. Hence, it is important that we see in to the future of each of these options. It is a form of foresight, one which can be gained from experience, working with experts and even a touch of the imaginative.

Reflect on past decisions. What worked? What didn't? There are important lessons that history can teach us in the now. Beware of being married to the past. The current situation is unique and it has its own variables to be factored in. There is a fine line between learning from the past and adjusting to today.

Engage with your team. The multi-faceted viewpoints can illuminate things you might have missed. You need to foster an environment of open discourse and generate a culture where employees feel comfortable sharing their perspectives. Between all these people, we have a collective intelligence that often points to the right action. Leadership is not about all of the answers; it is about having a system where the best answers have the ability to surface.

Examine the trade-offs of each choice. Quantify them if possible. Then again, not everything can be quantified. That being said, there are those risks of the more 'soft' and hard to measure nature that could really harm your team dynamics or culture which should then be incorporated within this initial weighting. Balance these qualitative factors with the quantitative ones for a 360-degree view.

Ethics and values should be at the heart of your evaluation. Choosing an option that trades against your principles can result in a temporary boost but, ultimately, also backfire. Live your values, and make choices consistent with the kind of leader you want others to experience working with. When approached like the actual kinematic deployment, configuration alignment helps ensure consistency and continuity—two necessities to keep a machine learning system from becoming cruft.

Before these options are laid out, take a moment to self-reflect. How do you feel via personal resonance with each option? Even the instincts (shaped by subconscious experiences and values) can, oh-so often, act as a compass when talio-logical analysis reaches its limits. Using that inner voice as a touchstone and not to the exclusion of other forms of evidence will result in leadership that is more open, genuine, and effective.

Key take-away: Lean towards decisiveness after doing the homework (and at times even when the homework is not as thorough). It is necessary to deliberate, but sometimes indecision can stall progress. Decide clearly and communicate your decision confidently to your team. This will convey the decisiveness of your choice, as well as build trust and provide a call to action.

Reflective leadership is a learning process that never ends. But every decision leads to you growing. Do not shy away from the lessons that every choice has to offer, and allow those lessons to improve the method by which you decide between opportunities in the future. As you continually reflect and act, through this iterative process, you will not only start making better decisions but eventually become a stronger, more inspiring leader.

Making Decisions

Act Quickly and Refine Later - When you are hesitating, ask yourself; "Whats the smallest action I can take right now?" Start small, then build.

Leadership is very much about choosing the right path when we are at a crossroads. This essential element of leadership is not just about choosing between two options, it is a chance for understanding one's values and instincts and the larger effect across affecting the team and organization.

Looking back in time, I ruminate over every decision ever weighed me down. Every decision felt like a smooth rock thrown into an undisturbed watering hole; the splash rippled across the surface for miles. The responsibility of making the "right" choice can be crippling, though it is precisely within these shades of gray where actual leadership is developed.

The most profound thing I learned though is how critical self awareness really can be. Being aware of ones' strengths, weaknesses and biases has a tremendous impact on choosing between yes or no. It is easy to get too influenced by personal preferences and past experiences, however realizing these influences can make us more balanced and objective. Those near-death moments are when I often confront my inner self, wondering why the hell am I working and trying to find a pinch of hope.

What is as equally needed, if not more important, is the gift of listening — to oneself, to others and to the elements. Aligning ourselves with a diversity of tones- and even those that may irritate us – will help to reveal blind spots expand perspectives. I can recall a moment when the dissent of one of my team members uncovered an issue that I had failed to address. It was a humbling experience but it highlighted the importance of voicing your opinion and having the courage to see things in a different light.

Leadership is seldom about black and white decisions. The majority are in gray, which tend to revolve around a tradeoff between logic and intuition. As much as we would like everything to be data-driven and as rational as possible, there is always going to be an intuitive, gut-feel side of decisions that cannot be ignored. I remember a turning point where data said something, but my heart was telling me otherwise. In that moment, the voice was reinforced by years of experience and wisdom... which led to a decision that ultimately paid off.

Accountability: What Drives the Decision-making. Engineered to deliver resultsWorkback from the user experience — This means owning not only the experience but also the outcome, victory or failure these are your stripes. I, of course, experienced my share of failure, but seeing myself learn from rather than stalling in response to these hiccups has been an essential part of my role as a leader. Admitting mistakes and being ready to pivot when required creates a trustful and resilient culture within the team.

Not only that but the impact of decisions goes beyond current returns. They are the ones that define the organizational culture and establish patterns for future actions. Each choice is a strand in the demanding tapestry of leadership, which binds in place all aspects of the head's values and vision. Awareness of this fact creates a feeling that makes someone think twice, not only what they get in the short run but also realizing that there will be some consequences sooner or later.

Decisions dance in the artwork of patience and timing, Too quick decisions might be omitting, while dwelling too much might make you lose a lot of chances. There is an art to rhythm, a time to act and a time to wait

— something that you only pick up through experience and mindfulness.

When I think about those aspects of the decision-making process, knowing that it does not stem from perfection but progression. It creates new challenges and learnings at each decision contributing to the evolving leader. Self-awareness, active listening, balanced judgment accountability and being mindful especially about timing also make a pathway of creating ways to make knowledgeable decisions.

Learning from Mistakes

"Good Judgment comes from experience, and experience comes from Bad judgment"

Mistakes are generally framed in the negative, as an unpleasant error to be prevented. But in the leadership universe, mistakes are more than inevitable; they are invaluable. Every mistake is a teacher, and from every teaching a leader is born. True growth is in these moments, in the reflection not the avoidance.

A good default reaction to a leader stumble is frustration or self-loathing. When instead you take a step back to look at what went wrong it becomes a stepping stone. This takes both humility and openness, two aspects leaders would do well to adopt! It is told, not just why this mistake occurred (the symptoms), but what led to the underlying conditions. What can be learned from it? How to Prevent Such Errors in the Future?

A maturing culture creates an atmosphere of continuous learning by promoting the recognition and discussion of errors. An environment where team members know so well that error is part of the road to greatness, and do not fear to take risks leading to inventions. By modelling this behaviour, Leaders essentially show us that mistakes are not the end of the road, but a detour to greater insights and improvements.

Imagine a project which doesn't deliver as intended. Rather than casting blame, a reflective leader will gather the team to deconstruct the failure. It is not an exercise of post-mortem but a process to understand the events that caused the difference. So, was there some kind of lost in translation? Were the goals unrealistic? Insufficient Resources or Capabilities on the Team This is done through a wider community of reflection where the team can discuss what worked and what did not work in order to get takeaways for future projects.

But personal imperfections are one of the most profound teachers in leadership. A leader who is brave enough to give his or her team permission to make mistakes is a truly great example. Engaging in vulnerability brings a team together. That a mistake is not a sign of weakness, but an opportunity for growth. By sharing their own experiences of failure and the lessons learned, leaders become more human in our eyes and promote a culture of openness and resilience.

One of those things is forgiving oneself and others as we learn from our mistakes. When the emphasis is too much on what was, and not enough on what will be — failure to progress is a natural riskOne of the most damaging obstacles for an organization to deal with is the concept that errors from the past cannot be forgiven. Unfortunately, leaders need to adopt a mindset that believes mistakes are part of learning. Thus, it gives a progressive approach by asking for the future and help in figuring out what to do not stunning over the damage done.

Solely rely on reflective practice to learn from your mistakes. Taking the time to reflect on our previous actions and their results can offer much-needed perspectives. Journaling, for example, can aid leaders in evaluating where they are succeeding and failing since it allows them to identify trends and work on better strategies. They NEVER forget a lesson they have learned from a mistake, because they are forced to reflect on it each and every day.

In the fluid and unpredictable world of leadership, mistakes are not incidents; they are moments. Approached with humility, these moments become transformative teaching ones. Leaders who demonstrate continuous improvement through inculcation of a learning from mistakes culture elevate their own skills and those in their teams. Beyond strengthening the individual leader, this approach actually expands the collective capacity of the organization altogether.

XI

Innovative Thinking for Leaders

Cultivating Creativity

How to Be a Hot Mess and a Genius at the Same Time! Because when your brain is a wild jungle of random thoughts, that's when the coolest ideas spring up—like a pop-up shop but with more chaos.

When exploring the Soul of leadership, it is impossible not to follow the lead of creativity. It is often the bit that signifies the start of idea generation for new projects and the offloading platform for teams to step into unknown territories. Creativity is not a magic/artistic ability, it's a skill that can be improved. A leader needs to learn what the environment is like for creativity to thrive within oneself and others.

At its core, innovation is the ability to challenge the norm. Leaders should challenge their teams to think in new ways, outside of the conventional norms. It means establishing a culture that accepts curiosity and understands that failure is a part of the learning process. In this era of psychological safety, team members feel confident enough to share their ideas and even make mistakes without being ridiculed or penalized.

The leader's task of honing creativity also includes setting the stage for a rich environment that amplifies learning. One way this happens is by various sources of insights that they are exposed to, for example, it could be through cross-functional team work or experience across different industries or continuous learning. By encouraging business team members to step out of their comfort zones and take on new experiences, fresh, maybe even quirky ideas can come forward that drive innovative solutions.

And also great creativity literally needs physical and mental space. This will allow a creative and experimental environment for your team so make sure you as leaders help and support it all the time. This might mean setting aside time for creative activities or creating environments that encourage collaboration and creative thinking. Advice: Flexitime and the opportunity to be unconventional can improve productivity immensely.

Growing creativity is not an act of isolation. It thrives in the sharing of ideas and working together. They should foster open channels of communication and establish an environment rooted in trust and a sense of mutual respect. The process should not be rigid and regular brainstorming sessions, workshops, and feedback loops can help to refine ideas into an actionable plan. They can gain some fresh and creative approaches from a team with varying experience, skills & knowledge.

And, to ensure the effectiveness of all these programs and for them to reach every household in India, the leaders will also have to lead by example. Managers can lead by example to open the mind of other staff members on solving problems and making decisions in a creative way. This requires a willingness to try things, take chances and figuring out what works by making mistakes. Leaders can model this same cultural element by exhibiting a dedication to continuous improvement and innovation.

Another important dimension for nurturing creativity is the acknowledgment and celebration of creative endeavours. Even the smallest contribution should not go unnoticed as any appreciation can be essential in morale boosting and encouragement to continue pushing boundaries. This can mean recognition in the form of public thank-you's at team meetings or it can be rewards that have a professional growth component.

In the end, fostering creativity is an endless road that demands faith in oneself and others over all judgments of success. It is like giving birth to a safe and nurturing womb for Ideas to grow in, where innovation blossoms as an inevitable republic of all collaborative action. With strategic implementation and a non-coercive leadership style, winning results and innovative breakthroughs can become part of the DNA of an organization.

Tip: Be brave enough to be bad at something new!

Encouraging Innovation in Teams

The Art of Making Your Team's Crazy Ideas Actually Work!

Innovation flourishes in an environment that allows for a creative path to success, as well as experimentation and the ability to take risks. As I think back on my success in coaching teams how to innovate, it proves that creating a culture in every team member feels responsible for being creative — will provide not just better innovative managers, but all these challenge loving people the ability to pursue freedom knowing they can land on their feet! Creating an environment where team members feel they can be creative and free in their thinking and ideas which will benefit the wider group is key to bring about the above.

One of the best ways to encourage innovation is by creating a sense of psychological safety in the team. When we feel a sense of safety to present our views without apprehension of being ridiculed or scolded, people would be more ready to bring forth new and weirder opinions. This cushion creates a space where team members can speak their minds, and try things without being paralyzingly afraid to fail. I remember all too well that on the most revolutionary projects it was this environment of trust and communication that truly created those groundbreaking ideas.

Another essential constituent is promoting variety of thought. By assembling people from different backgrounds, experiences and strains of thought, you can stir creativity and come up with innovative answers. As I look at my leadership journey, the teams that are not afraid to challenge derive better results by allowing for a wider perspective in problem solving. These conflicting view points are what often makes the breakthroughs in the room.

The spirit of innovation is primarily determined by leadership. Your confidence to step outside of the comfort zone motivates your team to go after their unknown. Looking back at leaders who have inspired me, it is these people who model a true desire to learn and some experimentation that are creating a ripple effect around them. And by one point of view this was good, their eagerness for innovation had a snowball effect on everyone else in the team to try more and break barriers.

This in turn is another essential input that can be provided like administrative assistance. Time: Innovation usually does not happen overnight (though there are those rare Eureka moments! From my experiences, the teams that I have worked with that were allowed to investigate new technologies, attend workshops and collaborate with people from the outside ran rings around those who didn't. So, the first importance for leaders is to make sure that their teams have the resources required to implement what they have thought.

Recognition and awards for your innovative efforts as well, also have some part in this. Recognizing and rewarding creative solutions reinforces how much innovation is valued. When I look back at the projects where we were highly successful, it was when teams that received acknowledgment for their in depth contributions, they just keep on innovating. This recognition may not always be monetary, often a simple Thank You for Giving is sufficient to foster the atmosphere of Innovation.

And the importance of continuous learning and development - It keeps the innovation intact by asking your team members to follow current trends in the industry, investing time in learning or further studies and lifelong learning. I have grown much in this way, and looking back, my best ideas surfaced when I was acquiring new knowledge through never-ending learning.

In other words, fostering innovation in teams means building a culture that rewards creativity, allows for failure and celebrates diverse thinking. It is leadership that motivates, resources that support, and a culture that appreciates lifelong learning. Thinking about these fundamentals, innovation cannot be just underestimated to a one-off – rather it is an ongoing journey where things like empathy as well as sacrifices also find their way into the day-to-day endeavours!

Implementing New Ideas

And so, leaders: Just as users are always looking for something new, you should also think of this as your opportunity to grow the next level in the game — the most satisfaction (and challenges!) will come when you conquer that boss level!

Remember, on a macro level you saw how your favorite Instagram dance went viral.. and everyone started doing it right? That's the kind of colorful vision that we need to start bringing into our workplace. A popular hashtag prompts momentum, and we need a culture that attracts and propels innovation in the same way. It implies creating a practice where experimentation is validated and failure is not viewed as a barrier, but instead perceived as an essential stage from which the creative path emerges — think of test driving an untried recipe that results in a kitchen disaster. So instead of getting dismayed, we discover new knowledge — what does and what does not work, which is how true innovation occurs in the end!

First of all, clear and effective communication lays the foundation to implement new ideas. Each member of the team should understand the vision and aim behind initiating a new strategy. Not only communication from top-down, but also better openness to validation — conversation. Getting team members to buy-in on the process becomes so much easier when they feel heard and valued.

One tactical option is to test new ideas in a limited form before they are applied throughout the entire organization. This lets him or her identify and address issues with little risk to the solution being developed. This is the point where really laying down all of your readings and feedback is imperative. What works well? What doesn't? Take these feedback and improve the concept & rework on it. This iterative loop not only helps you to get a better final outcome but it proves that you are ready for continuous improvement.

Resource allocation is also important. The implementation of new ideas is often costly, both in time, money and people. Leaders have to carefully balance these scarce resources, discarding them in an appropriate place and manner, such that the initiative gets its due share of support but carries on only at a cost less than other important operations. This might entail shifting existing resources or if need be accessing new ones. Open decision making and explaining why you took that call can help in keeping the faith of the team intact.

And Leadership is about leading by example through transition. Whenever you put in place new ideas, there are bound to be resistances and setbacks. The way a leader reacts to these challenges is going to have an impact on everyone in the team. Resiliency, adaptability and positive attitude attracts as well. Small wins should also be celebrated and contributions noticed throughout the journey. This serves to lift spirits but it also shores up buy-in to the new effort.

And create an empowering space with a safety net for every team member to try and err. Innovation is hardly ever a sequential process but one of experimentation, learning, and adjusting. What leaders need to do, is a place where failure can be seen as a learning process and not as a problem. This supports a growth mindset and allows for constant iteration — something that needs to be present for innovation at scale.

Success measurement of new ideas/community effort While it is impossible that every in-person event or trade show will have a positive ROI, you will greatly increase your chances by setting realistic goals from square one and tracking progress against these benchmarks at regular intervals. So its also a way not to get lost and make course correction along the way. Great leaders are not afraid to turn corners or give up their idea if it is not waning fruits. Indeed, this is a pragmatic way of making such that resources get allocated toward initiatives with the highest potential for impact.

Practically, to do is an evolving and continuous process. It is a delicate mix of visionary insight, strategic foresight and adaptive lateral leadership. These steps —building a culture of innovation, communication that is both disciplined and effective, piloting small but relevant initiatives using available resources judiciously, abiding by the principle of leading from the front and not delegating it until you become good at it and lastly having a learning bent — have helped me see through how we can make ideas work.

Overcoming Resistance

Resistance is a welcome — and inevitable — traveling companion along the way to leadership. We have all heard that the road to leadership is far from a straight line; it takes many twists and turns with countless hurdles which will challenge you along the way. As I reflected on my own experience, I realized that resistance is actually an incredibly powerful teacher.

Recognizing Resistance when confronted, the simplest step is admitting its existence. To deny or avoid the issue only helps it get a stronger hold. However, if we identify resistance then at least we can start to work on unravelling its roots. Resistance is often a result of fear, whether that be fear of change, failure or the unknown. So we, as leaders, should provide the environment to enable these fears make their way out and be dealt with. And key to both of these transactions is open communication and active listening.

This is one of the biggest lessons to take away from all of this: empathy. If we want to convince those resisting us, we serve to better put ourselves in their place

The ultimate result of which is, we human beings, allow to be bridged than walled. Empathy does not necessitate that we tubthump the viewpoints of others, but it does demand respect for feelings and acknowledgment. That builds credibility, trust and opens the door to collaboration.

Key Ingredient: Change is freakin slow, and resistance does not disappear overnight. Leaders need to learn the skill of patience. This is about allowing others the time and space to deal with and adjust to what has happened. This is a time to be more consistent in our actions and messaging. We need to show others that our dedication to the vision and the values which guide it are not negotiable.

Along the road, I have uncovered the magic of tiny victories. For an organization mired in the culture and habits of doing marketing in a certain way, big changes feel too scary and produce even more pushback. Breaking Goals Down Into Bite-sized Steps That You Can Realistically Hit Will Build Momentum One small victory leads to another, and the combined effect increases our confidence in our ability to achieve progressive steps forward. By celebrating even the smallest of wins, this breeds a culture of positivity and positivity encourages more action.

There is no way around transparency when it comes to addressing resistance. Mistrust and opposition can grow in environments with hidden agendas and lack of clarity. When we are open with our intentions, plans and obstacles, we create a space for others to come along with us in the process. This transparency helps to build ownership and accountability — so we are all in the trenches together.

Change also requires immense adaptability. Usually that resistance is also a symptom of something not working correctly. Effective leadership means that you will need to go back again and again and review your strategies in light of feedback, circumstances or both. Being flexible is not necessarily a sign of weakness but more the case towards finding the most optimal path forward.

In the end, resistance is a people problem. One is not a leader alone, leadership is collaboratively having the backing and cooperation to facilitate another. When we invest in relationships, we are investing in a solid base of trust and mutual respect that can help our resistance stand up to the hard work and strong winds of change.

After thinking all these perspectives, it seems resistance is not a radical hurdle of leadership but resides as its essential part. When we encounter and defeat resistance, we grow as leaders (and as human beings). It is by no means easy but it is also filled with moments of growth and change!

Tip - The 'never give up' mindset is overrated, knowing when to quit the wrong path and pivot is what leads to real breakthroughs.

Measuring Innovation Success

Which crazy idea really worked? As you probably imagine, once you are caught up in the intricacies of leadership — sensing the nuances both subtly and starkly at times — measuring innovation success goes without saying.

Simply telling other people to use their imagination isn't enough; as leaders, we must also have the insight to assess its impact. We follow a careful mix of quantitative metrics and qualitative insights to see if our innovations aren't just new, but are also helpful.

The first layer is the hard metrics; The increase in revenue, its market share and the return on investment are good attributes of an innovation evaluation. These economic indicators tell if an idea has turned a profit. But falling back to these on their own can be deceptive. An innovation may produce limited financial returns to start with, and yet over the long term, could be of considerable strategic worth. This is why balance becomes so important.

Now enter the world of customer feedback. Field level indicators such as customer satisfaction scores, Net Promoter Scores (NPS) and user engagement metrics offer a point of view into how innovations are resonating in the market. So a saleable product or service may be financially successful, but if it doesn't connect with customers about saving the earth then its sustainability is suspect. It gives a much more detailed understanding of what needs to be improved or where to pivot.

Another important feature is Employee engagement This assists in creating an innovative culture where employees believe their contributions matter. Establish surveys and feedback mechanisms to measure the satisfaction and productivity impact of innovational initiatives Innovation of increased qualityHigher and more inventive ideas are generally a byproduct when members are emotionally invested in the innovation process.

Also, think about how innovations strategically relate. Even if an idea is one-of-a-kind, it loses its relevance when it deviates from the organizations vision and goals. Measuring innovation against strategic fit ensures that resources go to projects that push the organization forward. It requires ongoing exams and alterations, consistent with the innovation pipeline on course in general.

The process of the innovation itself begs greater scrutiny. Second, operational metrics (e.g. time-to-market and development cycle efficiency) measure innovation from another angle. All these can be made faster with optimizations, bringing down the iteration time and making it a better product. Equally important, we need to establish a culture where well thought out risks are acceptable and where failures become valuable learning experiences. Every defeat adds strength, shapes the innovation process and redefines how you innovate.

One must also take into account the non tangible gains that innovation has to offer. From a less tangible but still highly meaningful perspective, they serve as a normative brand-building—an industry badge of honor, talent-magnetizing proof of the tremendous IP generation housed within. These additional components raise the status of the organization and create an avenue for mutual growth. Incorporating these soft measures gives more holistic view on how well innovation success is evaluated.

Finally, peer benchmarking provides useful information. Contextualize Your Innovation Metrics with Industry Benchmarks and Competitor based insights It tells you what you are good in and what can be improved. This outside point of view may provide the impetus to change your innovation strategy.

It is as if the determination of success in innovation where it not belongs to one scope of measurement. It takes a blend of monetary and non-monetary measures based on customer information, employee feedback, strategic weaponisation, process improvement activities and brand value propositions. Leaders who take a strategic perspective can make sure that their innovation work is not only nimble but also sticky, meaning it stays on target and contributes to the organization's longer term view. By engaging in this strategic reflection, leaders can continuously improve their plans and practices that promote innovation leading the way to significant change.

XII

Leading with Integrity

Understanding Integrity

It is the Wi-Fi that binds together every other leadership characteristic and enables them to operate. Your demeanor, how you carry yourself says a lot louder what why and how do your actions. If you lack of integrity then nothing clicks!

Integrity-wise, remember that honesty is one of the divine lacks spirit and ethics have nothing to do with each other. Although telling the truth is a part of integrity, integrity encompasses so much more than that. Authenticity means being honest to oneself and others, a concept where you do exactly as you say which aligns your actions with values. The alignment that represents the necessary pre-condition for trust and respect from those we lead over time, not just by fear or adulation — is something of an infrastructure for real leadership.

Think about the tremendous impact of leaders which lasts on us. And it remembers the manner in which they carried themselves, too. And by showing their dedication to what they believe even in the presence of trials tells you a whole lot. Great leaders follow that unerring guidepost of one's right direction. It shows their integrity, an attribute that cannot be faked.

Integrity, in the leadership sphere and elsewhere, takes many forms. The transparency in the communication of a leader where they have no hidden agendas, It is seen in the justice by which choices are structured and in the way we honor as well as accord equal value to each other. That then reflects in accountability, taking the blame for things gone wrong; it is learning from mistakes. In so doing, they establish a reverberating pulse which defines the character and principles of those teams/organizations.

Integrity also encourages honesty in others. It establishes a bar, a bar to which others will aspire. The team members feel safe by knowing that their leader is going to do the best thing on their behalf with the help of a good moral compass. Trust is the foundation of teamwork and collaboration, enabling success in teams.

But it can be a daunting task to cling onto your values SOMETIMES, LEADERS ARE FACED WITH THE DIFFICULT DECISION: DO WHAT IS EASY OR DO WHAT IS RIGHT. It is in these moments that integrity is tested. It takes a lot of courage and kind of bravery to stand up for your values, even when it is hard or does not align with the popular opinion. And it requires a keen awareness of what your values really are, and the self-control to stick with them when everyone else around you is not.

Continue your journey of getting what it is that integrity means. This takes lots of self reflection and openness to growth. Leaders need to check in with themselves that their actions and decisions line up with their values. It is not a sign of weakness to do this introspection, really it is a sign of strength as there must be personal growth before you can professional grow.

Integrity is the beacon, guiding our way in the never-ending journey of learning and leading. It lights the path, making sure that every step we make is based on reality and existence. The further one develops in leadership, the more we understand that integrity is everything. It is the rock upon which trust, respect and true leadership are formed – a reaffirmation of the continued strength of leading with your values first.

Tip : Know when to quit - 'Never Give Up' mindset is sometimes overrated. Knowing when to quit the wrong path cuts your losses and leads you to real breakthroughs. Strategic quitting is also a superpower!

Building Trust

Trust: The Ultimate Leadership Hack (No Filter Needed!)

Trust is the foundation of effective leadership. I think back on my own career, and I know that trust has been central to every team environment I have ever led. It takes something bigger: working at it consistently, truly wanting to do this properly and letting it all out — naked.

That is one of the first lessons to learn when we talk about trust. Transparency. When you are a leader that is open with your decisions, motivations and even to some extent you mistakes, what ensues is an environment where team members feel safe and valued. I can recall a time I had to make a tough decision that did not jive with the thinking of my team. I did not just enforce it I explained the reasoning for it. Despite the initial resistance, this transparency led to a new level of comprehension and subsequently — trust.

Another important question, of course, is listening. It's not about listening to receive words but understanding what your team is really concerned, thinking and feeling. A few jobs ago, I worked with someone who was frequently very silent in meetings. His silence was easy to miss, but I chose to speak with him one-on-one. Through that conversation, I learned that he had some really important insights and ideas, but was just not comfortable voicing those in front of a bigger audience. Through providing a voice and space, I earned his trust and unlocked potential creativity and innovation for the team.

All about walking and talking the same. People need to ensure that they can trust their leader. Harking back to my career, there were definitely moments where such small act of consistent behaviour (e.g. always starting meetings on time, or delivering what I say we will) established a foundation of trust. Slowly chipping away with smaller things, is usually more impressive than one huge clean house.

Trust is a function of empathy. This human level of exposure and reciprocity extends far outside the confines of a typical professional working relationship. There was a time in my career that I will never forget, and I say that with all seriousness. It was in this human-to-human conversation that I gave permission for both sides to express their fears and anxieties, even me as the manager — mutual reinforcement was born. This empathy helped us sail through the harsh phase and it built a very strong bond of trust within the team.

It helps keep me accountable as well!! Owning up to your mistakes and willing responsibility is very empowering. In the midst of descending on a project, there was one time I made an awful mistake from a strategic point of view which consumed many hours of our precious time. So I fessed up in front of the team — instead of trying to blame others. This act of accountability won the admiration of their peers and fostered a culture based on fearlessness, allowing people to be bold, make mistakes and grow.

Trust, as you might remind us all is a two-way street; it has to be given and received. You essentially empower your team by showing (not just saying) you trust them and their capabilities. I remember waiting an important job out to a brand-new team member. Believing in her ability, and trusting her to deliver elevated performance, and that is what happened as well. It serves as a reminder of what people will do in response to trust.

Looking back on those experiences, it is obvious that trust is not something you create one time and then are done. It takes time, regularity and honest regard for the health of your team. Trust is what turns a group of individuals into one formidable force to conquer any challenge faced.

Tip: "Trust me" - This may come across a bit defensive giving way to question your reliability, it can feel like you are asking for trust rather than earning it. Instead, say: "Here is why I believe this approach is right"

Consistency in Actions

The importance of consistency in anyone's journey as a leader is monumental. It is not just about the big acts or drama like speeches that make you a leader, its always act of yours — your day to day action that speaks for who you are. Trust is the foundation for good leadership and consistent action fosters trust. It helps everyone on your team to find a common ground and focus on doing their best with the comfort of knowing what you can expect from them (continuous delivery/transparency is key, emotionally and in product development) in return.

But mainly, consistency is like the thread that runs throughout the cloth of your leadership. It is these small choices we make every single day that stack together over time to form one big picture. Consistently following through on your promises allows for trust in your team that you are reliable. This type of reliability breeds dependability directly within the team. Eventually, folks start to model what they see and before you know it everyone values consistency.

Think of a room where the light switch turns on sixty percent of the time, or only sometimes. You'd cautiously tread the line each time. Leadership is no different. They're going to hesitate if they question how you'll respond to their actions. This uncertainty is eliminated by consistency. And it lets your team do their work without second-guessing what you are going to do next.

However, consistency should never mean rigidity. It is to strike that balance between changing and not changing — where you change with more information or as the environment changes, while staying aligned with your fundamental core values. (There is some room for flexibility in leadership, but you need consistency and a sound set of cores to build everything off of. A leader is truly a force to reckon with if he can strike this balance of being firm and flexible at the same time.

Also, the importance of keeping to your word ties directly into accountability as well - The Most Powerful Statement for a Leader to Make — Medium It means that you are not greater than the law, and all possess an equivalent responsibility to a joint progress. When your team is held accountable at this level they may draw more ownership from themselves thus enabling them to execute their roles at the highest of levels and committing to each tasks as if it were theirs.

Consistency in actions also helps greatly during uncertain times. Your team will look to you for guidance when it is unclear which way forward should be taken. When they have seen you act consistently in the past, they can trust that you know how to overcome adversity. It will serve also as a stabilizing that assists the team in remaining committed and focused during turbulent times.

It is also vital to appreciate the fact that consistency itself is a process, not a place you can reach. It takes work, every single day and self reflection. You will slip up, and that is great too. The key is your dedication to start over and stay the course now. Writing reflections of what you did on a daily basis, your week and month could help see where you are missing the mark which allows to self-correct.

At its essence, being consistent in practice is really about establishing a reliable and trusted presence with your team. This is about the standard you have for yourself and living to it, daily. Your steadfast commitment to the process of regular improvement will further grow your reputation and influence others to follow in kind.

Ethical Decision-Making

Leading with Ethics: It's Like Choosing a Salad Over Fries—Hard, but Your Team Will Thank You Later!

Ethics may seem like something out of a fiction novel to many, however in leadership they are very real and applied on the spot. Each decision reverberates out, changing the way team members feel about their lives and work, eroding trust with stakeholders and modeling culture for a company. And the problem is that we easily fall into the daily requirements and pressures, never remembering to make a continuous and deliberate effort to act ethically, which are true leadership positions.

Self-awareness is one of the initial steps in an ethical decision. This is true of our leaders as well, the more one for knows his or her values bias and motivation the better. This self-awareness is a compass that steers decisions when in doubt. But leaders who lack this introspection may feel that external pressures or personal gain pull them in directions that are not right nor are just. Reflective leaders stop themselves to understand their ethical frameworks and how they feel that this way influences their decisions.

Another cornerstone is transparency. When decisions are made behind closed doors with no input, or even explanation, deceit and distrust is bred. Core protocols and why decisions are made introduce an open line of tell that generates credibility. It may not always be about consensus, but it is to make the decision-making process transparent and understandable. It promotes a more accountable system and can also automatically generate higher quality, all encompassing decisions by virtue of diverse perspectives.

One of the most important things to take into consideration is how your decisions affect everybody else. Ethical leaders do not limit themselves to the immediate consequences but wilful take the long view of other people, communities and as well as ecological systems. They inquire among themselves, how does our actions mirrors the values and purpose of this organization. This 360-degree view helps ensure that the decisions we make are not just in the interests of immediate gains, but for the overall betterment of humanity.

What also comes with accountable leadership are a number of grey ethical areas: those pressing situations where it is unclear which path is the right one to take. In such situations it is crucial to pull from an established ethical framework and consult with trusted advisors. Hearing from others can offer fresh view points and assist with the confusion of the dilemma. It is in these difficult times that a leader will show his true colors.

The exercise of ethical decision–making requires courage Doing the right thing is often difficult, even when it is unpopular or carries personal risk, because courage to act for justice requires a collective willingness. Leaders with high moral standards must take these positions, as their integrity and the trust of their team depend on it. This courage is what often, leads to the separation of good leaders from great ones.

There is nothing more important than empathy. Compassionate and knowledgeable leadership will draw from awareness of the needs and losses felt by others towards more equitable decision making. Real compassion, the application of this form of honesty and insight when it counts, is a learned behavior that leads to better leaders acting in more human ways.

Ethical decision-making is not a product, but an on-going journey. It demands constant thinking, learning and adjusting. Because our environment is in constant flux, with new data-to-decide coming at us every second, our leaders have to be vigilant; they have to always reevaluate their decisions and their results. Engaging in these behaviors fosters a culture of ethical leadership that resonates with third-party organizations, helps to build an ethical, value-based organization and encourages others to act with integrity.

Lastly, making ethically sound decisions should be the aim, not just avoiding wrongdoing. It is from willingly seeking to make a positive difference — to working towards outcomes that bring more love and power, and leading in a way that is perpetually congruent with our highest values. Now that is true leadership.

Role Models of Integrity

In a discussion about leadership the essence of which is its moral strength, no one should ignore the enormous influence on young future leaders who are an example of integrity. More often than not overlooked, these people are the very paradigm of honesty and transparency who with an ethical behavior serve as lighthouse to those charting through the maze of leadership. It is not their actions alone but a deeply principled dedication to those ideals that effectuates the influence of these entrepreneurs on minds and hearts.

Think of the steadfast integrity shown by a mentor who does stand for what is right, despite all difficult considerations. By standing up to the tough, dirty work of telling the truth (or resisting half-truths), they create a trust and respect engine in their orbit. Watching this behaviour, you find out what leadership really means: it is not an excuse to break rules when the odds are against you, but having a spine of steel instead. A mentor is far less effective if they do not model such behavior, because the integrity of his/her word is THE foundation for sustainable leadership.

Business leaders who lead with virtue and integrity changes whole organizations. They are transparent in their decision-making processes and they ensure that their employees and partners have a decent life. This, in turn boost the morale of not only the workforce but by doing so they build a work force that is loyal and motivated. The best outcome happens when workers are inspired by the ethical behavior of their leader, and these values permeate both work and personal life. And this, in turn, can create a new culture of honesty throughout the organization by osmosis (the so-called halo effect.)

Looking back at our predecessors who are influential historical personalities, there exists the courageous and honest leader who has withstood the test of time. We can think of figures like Mahatma Gandhi, and Nelson Mandela — great leaders dealing with the biggest of challenges would not compromise on their basic principles. People — these men and women had so much conviction, embedded in morality and justice. These role models demonstrate that integrity is not a fixed quality but operates as a dynamic, gritty journey, one in which courage and fortitude are frequently necessary.

A striking example of integrity role models can be glimpsed in everyday life. For example, a teacher who resists external pressure from parents to change children's grades or a bureaucrat who reports corruption despite the danger involved or someone being genuinely honest when the truth is razed. These adults show by their deeds that integrity is not a great act but a small habit. We see how all decisions create an opportunity for integrity, no matter what the size of our examples.

Those who aspire to lead should seek out these models and learn from them. Their behavior, motivations and impact all create powerful lessons. The answer is to observe and reflect again and again, over these observations until the realization sinks in: leadership with integrity.

Leadership is fundamentally about leading others toward a common vision. But without integrity, it is probably going to be a short-lived vision. Acts of integrity are pounded out as a source of hope, that ethical leadership is possible and necessary. That forces us to be our best selves, which demands that we show up with authenticity and integrity. In their light, we understand that leadership is not about forcing followers but inspiring them, a process in which respect is gained through right and steadfast instructions.

XIII
Adapting to Change

Embracing Change

Change Is Scary, But So Is My 6 AM Alarm—Let's Embrace the Chaos!

Life changes all the time, and while it should be something that we are used to, it usually puts us off and scares us at first. For leaders, being able to gate change is as much a need as it is something good. Looking back at my own life, there were times when change feels almost impossible. Yet, it was during these times of deep despair that the greatest personal and professional growth took place.

The first step to adjusting to change is acknowledging that its a reality. Change is part of nearly everything in our lives, whether it be within the markets we participate in, structural organizational changes, or technological advancements. Leaders who grasp this are able to be proactive instead of reactive. This is not about future-guessing but rather being flexible and ready for new opportunities.

Back when I was early in my career, I often resisted change. I worshiped certainty and predictability as the bedrock of good leadership. But, I shortly came to understand that maintaining the standing was not only impracticable but also stifling. The world outside is constantly changing and you need to evolve in order to become an effective leader.

One key moment for me was when my organization underwent a massive technological reset. Change was happening, and it was good to a certain extent...to see the old systems we had become so accustomed to evolving into something new. There was a lot of pushback from the team I am on, myself included. In each, the new systems were such they needed a whole different kind of skillset to manage and operated so differently from prior methods that long-standing habits had to be entirely forsaken. But the more I understood and learned about this process, the more I saw the upside. These new systems for the management of the infrastructure helped us clean up our processes, increase automated communication, and boost our overall productivity.

It was a life lesson learned, change is hard but it often brings improvement. It pushed me to the limit, so I had to learn new skills. It was a major factor in reinforcing the value of having a good attitude. Then I started to think of change as an opportunity to learn and grow, instead of something against me.

Communication is a second key factor in preparing to navigate change. There are more keep alive techniques that you will need to do as a leader. First and foremost, communicate! Your changes will have a higher success rate if your teams are well-informed and can relate to them. During the tech refresh, I ensured that my team continued to gain visibility of what we were working towards and what we would get out of it. Such openness eliminated some of the fear and resulted in a sense of partnership.

Based on these experiences, I realise now that we need to build a culture of adaptability and fluidity. This culture is primarily shaped by leadership. Leaders can model adaptability and support their teams through change, demonstrating by example that transformation is an integral part of being human.

So, change is not to be avoided but it should be utilized in itself. We gain new strengths, we learn new skills and unlock new opportunities when we change. Our job as leaders is to navigate our teams through these changes, helping them find the gift in every challenge. This allows for continued growth and success, where that adaptability we instill in our team permeates throughout the organization.

Leading Through Uncertainty

To lead is to sail, and sailing uncertain waters requires more than just a steady hand; it takes a willingness to change course and an uncompromising commitment to who you are. I reflect back on times in my own life when the way ahead was completely lost in the mist and everything I did felt like a step into darkness. That is when real leadership is born.

But there is a very fond memory of my early career. I was managing a team through a major organizational restructuring. The company made the decision to pivot and the subsequent uncertainty was in the air. Employee fears were high, productivity tanked, rumors ran rampant. I saw how uncertain it was and as the leader I felt the crush of these uncertainties on me. I needed to lead my team through this time of crisis but, I also couldn´t lose sight of our tasks.

Cracking the code of Communication became my anchor. What I realized was people tend to fill in the blanks when there is not enough information with fears and imagined worse case scenarios. So I tried to be as open and transparent with my reasons and what evidence I did or didn't have. The openness helped in building the trust and solidarity within the team. We were not alone and collectively trembling with the uncertainty of the future.

In addition, it was key to uphold the cornerstone of what we were about. With external change, internal similarities provide stability. I urged my team to reflect upon our mission and values, to remember why we were there in the first place. This gave us a mission and even in moments when the longer term may not have been clear,

He said flexibility was also important. Rigid behaviours in a moment of uncertainty can be damaging. I learned to approach things with an open but pragmatic mind, behaviour helped by being willing to pivot when needed and then encourage my team to do the same. This kind of thinking not only enabled us to pivot quickly and efficiently but it also created a culture of innovation and resilience.

Empathy Empathy was easily one of the more profound things I learnt from this period. The way people process uncertainty is great, and as a leader of ateam it is important to identify and mitigate the ways inwhich un-certainty is interpreted. I listened to what my team had to say, I quickly validated their feelings and provided support where it was called for. Not only did this reduce some of the pressure, but it also promoted team unity.

On reflection on these experiences I understand that leading through uncertainty is not about knowing everything or making the right decisions. It is about being there, being honest, and being flexible. At the end of the day, it is about staying true to your values and weathering the storm with your team. This is remembering that fear and uncertainty should always be present in leadership and this darkest hour will bring the biggest opportunities for growth & transformation.

Ultimately, leading in uncertainty is a measure of your resilience and dedication to your guys. It is a craft that takes practice, introspection and the ability to both take directions from yourself and evolve filtering it out. The direction may not always be obvious, but the road is priceless educator.

Flexibility in Leadership

Although flexibility in leadership is something that should never be undervalued, it is clearly a fundamental aspect of good management. It is critical that leaders be capable of adjusting amidst the frenetic pace and volatility in response to sudden changes. Certainly, reading flexibility in other journals and reflecting upon my lived experiences reveals plenty of what-might-have-happened mistakes if I was just a tiny bit more rigid.

A major example hails from a project over which I was in charge just a few years ago. When our team had strict deadlines to launch a new product. We started out with a long and seemed perfect plan. But as it turns out, when we got deeper into the project, a number of unexpected difficulties popped up. A critical supplier did not deliver, and unforeseen changes occurred with market conditions. If we had not been more flexible, the project would have crashed and burned. We reorganized, reformulated our strategies, we found other sources! The project was saved, a product launched, and the solution made robust by this flexibility.

Considering this, what we can see is when we speak of leadership being flexible- it goes parallel to the fact that adaptation with plans changing is not just about being a leader[event] in reality. This is about creating an environment where your team feels they are in a position to say what might be wrong provide some answers of another way this could work. In return, leaders are able to tap into the collective intelligence and creativity of their teams. According to this affirmative, more often than not a team approach results in creative solutions that otherwise even an experienced individual might fail to identify.

And: of course, flexibility requires humility. Leaders need to accept that they do not always know best and be open to learning from others. Especially if you are a high-flyer who is used to being the one with the answers. And it is that willingness to learn and grow that separates great leaders from good leaders.

For another example, at the time I was working on a team that had morale issues. The instinct was to apply a suite of rigid performance metrics and top-down accountability. Thing is: A quick read may have suggested efforts not enough, and they were probably trying to cover all the time worked on extra stuff into overtime. After speaking with team members, real reason it was happening = not feeling enforced and a lack of voice heard. Sure enough, by moving the goalposts from metrics to morale, we were able to find a lot of uplift. One such shift in methodology took agility and a readiness to abandon the traditional management dance.

But it also means allowing for flexibility in the leadership journey – be that at an organizational or a personal level. In terms of learning and growth, this also means the leader has to be open to evolve his/her own skills and perspectives. The process might include finding a mentor, going to workshops or it may just mean being open to feedback. Taking place in an organism of change, personal growth is just that: an ongoing process, so he flexibility is unlikely to keep more irrelevant dinosaurs are best a step behind where they could have been. or Flexibility only the most effectively responds to ever-evolving surrounding weAs leadersgeschickte people you know crazy well oncEinmal The constant motions beschwört eingegreifen.

One of the biggest takeaways for me has been that flexibility does NOT equal lack of vision or direction. However, it is also about having a vision and being open to the many ways with which you might be able to realise that vision. This might sound like a paradox, but it is all about mixing determination of goals with flexibility in approach.

During times of change, flexibility in leadership means responsiveness and not reactivity. This is in short building a culture out of change, rather than running away from it. Such a mentality enables leaders to have agility and resilience in the complexities of contemporary business. In light of my experiences, it is clear to me that being flexible is not a tactic but a quintessential part of good leadership.

Supporting Your Team

Supporting a team is more than just giving resources or setting targets, it is to create an environment where every member can learn and motivate each other. Instead it starts with the recognition that each person comes to work equipped with a different set of skills, insights, and experiences. These unique qualities are needed to create a strong team and embracing them is essential.

Active listening is one of the best ways that you can be there for your team. All this boils down to is actually listening to what your team members have to say instead of just waiting for your chance to talk. This means questioning, getting to clarity, and acting with empathy. This is also critical to a more collaborative and innovative team, when team members feel that their voice is heard.

Another crucial part of helping your team is to foster open communication. Establish an open culture where team members feel safe speaking out — not being judged or retaliated against for sharing their opinion. Regular check-ins, team meetings, and one-on-one conversations go a long way in achieving this. While not an earth-shattering revelation, making this principle the backbone of your interactions fosters a sense of openness and fuels team relationships.

It is a means to ensuring both personal growth and professional development Give feedback on behaviors and outcomes — not the person. One of the biggest points to make when giving feedback is clarity, brevity and support — emphasising both where they did well, but also how areas can be improved. Also, be willing to accept feedback from team members. It also proves that you respect their opinions and believe in continuous improvement.

Empowerment // This is another key ingredient of team support. Have faith on your team and let them decide and manage their work. Give them the tools and learning they need to be successful. As a result, empowerment can create an environment of autonomy and accountability, which can drive motivation and job satisfaction. It also drive innovation and problem solving as everyone feels assured that they have the ability to contribute to the success of their team.

Acknowledgment and recognition is one of the best ways to foster your team. Celebrate accomplishments, no matter how minor, and respect the members of your team. This can be through verbal praise, written notes or through public recognition during team meetings. Recognizing and celebrating success means more than just adding a tick against one of your goals to be achieved — it can also boost morale, whilst reinforcing good behaviours which will continue to push the team towards that same pursuit of excellence.

Encouraging Team Growth and Development Provide training programs and workshops along with offering level-appropriate resources to facilitate the continuous learning. Encourage team members to set and achieve personal professional goals. You are both upskilling them while also displaying your willingness to invest in their future.

Finally, you will need to build an environment that is conducive to helping your team. Create a respectful, coactive, and inclusive atmosphere within the company. Lead your team to assist one another, learn, and strive towards the same objectives. Positive team culture increases job satisfaction among employees, decrease stress rate in the teams and boost overall team performance.

Supporting them is an ongoing journey that involves commitment, empathy and genuinely wanting to see your team thrive. An environment that is conducive to your team excelling, can be established through active listening, open communication, constructive feedback, empowering staff members, acknowledgment of achievements and accolades offered for growth with a positive enforcive culture.

Learning from Change

Change is a part of life and often the surprise teacher. How effectively and how much we improve also will largely depend on the extent to which we can learn from change as leaders. Looking back, it's clear that valuable insights often come when the earth shakes beneath one's feet. Difficult as they are, these moments of failure can act as a great catalyst for personal and professional growth.

Think about a time when there was a big change at your professional place of employment. For some, maybe it was the restructuring, a new team or an unanticipated market change. At first, implementation of these measures may cause discomfort or confusion. Our natural instinct as humans is to want to hold onto the known and familiar way of doing things. It is true that this was a mild conspiracy and the sign of a truly adaptable leader its ability to navigate these channels with curiosity and openness.

They realised the importance of asking the right question in those moments. What can this change tell us about the ways we are doing things today? But what are the untapped potential opportunities in this disruption? So we consider change as a scary monster that we battle instead of an opportunity to learn — embracing it opens up unique roads to growth. It tips the scales of despair to hopelessness and shifts the thinking from just surviving to proactively adapting.

In thinking back on my own experiences, I could go on and on with so many examples of where discomfort at first evolved into learnings. Consider, for example, that time a valued team member walked out your door. The initial response will probably be one of deprivation and a worry, what next? That said, it can also provide a healthy scrutiny on team dynamics, individual roles and how a different type of work batch should trickle its way down in the form of newfound delegation. Usually, it comes some underlying powerbase / inefficiency or cracks that had been around but unnoticed.

But due to outside forces — market trends, changes in technology — a good leader must also be an informed and tactical one. This is even more true with the rapid pace of technological change requiring constant learning and adjustment. When leaders take time to learn new tools and methodologies it adds another level to their skill sets as well serving as inspiration for their teams.

Feedback — Feedback is arguably the next most important part of learning from change. Formal and informal feedback loops are key sources of how changes are being received and put into practice. Over time, this ongoing dialogue helps leaders learn to pivot strategy as it is happening—and enables the creation of a culture of shared learning. This will remind team members to share what they perceive and think, which enhance decision-making inclusiveness as well.

Change also places an emphasis on the importance of emotional intelligence. To effectively lead during times of change, you need to be highly aware of your own emotional state and the emotions of others. Now, these are the essential tools to have; empathy, patience, and clear communication. The more leaders recognize and allow for emotional responses to a change, the stronger their teams will be—more effective and better prepared—for the steps that are to come.

Thinking back on those experiences clearly the ability to learn from change is not only a static capability but more of an iterative function. To really WORK at it — force them to get better involves constant self-evaluation, willingness to change and openness to new perspectives To develop this perspective as leaders strengthens our own abilities while also modeling for those we lead.

Leadership, at its core, is a journey of learning. Every change, every challenge brings its own lesson. And today when we let change teach, life becomes a teacher and in doing so, as teachers navigate the complexity of leadership more skillfully and naturally makes us more available- resilient and most importantly inspiring.

XIV

Mentoring and Coaching Others

The Role of a Mentor

Mentorship in its core is a fragile and deep dance of past an future. This is a bond that goes beyond just teaching, it ties in threads of wisdom and motivation along with steering. Upon contemplation of the role we serve as mentors, it is evident that our functionality extends well beyond knowledge transfer...our privilege goes further to only nurturing possibilities.

The mentor is a light guiding you in the rite of passage towards your professional and personal growth. This light not only shines our path, but also reflects back rays of warmth onto the mentee and their own talents and passions that they had lost a sense to or never seen. Mentors are then not just sharing what they know but really listening, observing, and responding to what their mentee needs.

The most profound mentors in my life have been those who actually cared about the person behind the professional. They asked me questions, that went to core of my beliefs, and softly pushed me just out of my comfort zone. Their feedback sometimes was hard to hear, although it always came from a place of knowing my capabilities and wanting the best for me.

From the perspective of a mentor, part of your function is to act as a mirror; allowing your mentee to see where they are strong and weak. The idea of this reflection is not to be fault finding by nature but pointing out ways we can improve ourselves in our life journey. The key is to create a mindset that sees challenges as stepping stones instead of roadblocks. If a mentor can enable this shift in perspective he will have truly made a difference which is what makes all the difference between success and failure.

Mentoring: Someone who offers you advice or provides guidance as a mentor also means to act as a sounding board. This is the space where they can open up without being judged by anyone. Such an open dialogue is essential for the mentee, in order to be prompted to deep critical and creative thinking. Similarly, the mentor offers insights and perspectives that expand what is in reach for the mentee, making them aware of possibilities they may not have entertained.

Mentorship Relationship....Trust is the Foundation of this Relationship Without that, the advice given could sound empty and untrustworthy. Earning this trust takes time, and not just a shared connection, but also patience and true care in your mentee's well-being. I think the most important characteristic of fatherhood is just being there — showing up, both physically and emotionally. It is in this trust where the mentee can take risks, err and learn from their mistakes while knowing they always have someone rooting for them on the other end of the line.

As I look back upon the mentors who helped to lead me down my path, I see that lessons not only stem from their exact words. My parents gave me a feeling of confidence that served as the backbone to all of my ambitions. In everything I do, they are there -- my guide in adversity, the spark that encourages me to push through obstacles with grace and ease, and the example of love that I work every day to express to those around me.

A mentor is someone who has the power to determine futures, build confidence and plant a seed for growth. This is a duty that involves not only subject matter expertise but also empathy, patience and a real desire to help others succeed. This deep student-mentor bond showcases the eternal quality of human relations and what we are all possible of when properly guided by a thoughtful mentor.

Effective Coaching Techniques

Coaching is an art, a fine balance between enabling and self sufficiency. It is appreciating that every person has a different set of random challenges and secret weapons, and designing our methods around how we might help the most black people come into themselves. The crux of great coaching is a solid rapport built on trust, recognition and decent correspondence. Its not about giving directions, but inspiring self-awareness and growth.

Active listening is the basis of powerful coaching. It goes beyond just listening; it is a matter of seeking the meaning behindocabulary. When you listen very closely a coach can detect fine signals and unspoken ideas that are not invited to the surface just yet. This profound listening creates a safe space where people feel appreciated and seen, which leads to them opening up even more.

Another keystone in an effective coaching approach is asking powerful open-ended questions. This gets them thinking, assumptions are questioned, and insights are rich. We also wrote our questions to where receiving yes or no responses would not work — these were written to/ or around exploration and self-reflection. Selling three things instead of asking: "What do you think the biggest challenge is for you?" or "how would you do things differently in this situation? encourage critical thinking, personal insight.

Giving constructive feedback is also important. She told the journalists that negative feedback must be specific, objective, and targeted at conduct instead of individuals. Where you should showcase strengths and success, but also identify opportunities for growth. My intention, is to bring a neutral view which will inspire us in the right direction so that it compels you further with practical actions. Feedback is a conversation not a talk, that challenges ones thinking and promotes response.

Coaching involves setting clear and practical goals. Goals give you direction and purpose. First, they should be SMART (specific, measurable, achievable, relevant and time-bound) goals. When individuals have a clear goal, they are more engaged and motivated and withstood the accurate road map to measure progress or celebrate small milestones as they achieve them. It is key to have individuals involved in the setting of 2uC goals, so they are meaningful and aligned with individual aspirations and values.

The tool of involving self-reflection and self-assessment is very powerful in coaching. It helps people in their development to own it and to be able to see how far they have come. It allows them to capitalize on what they are good at, understand where they can improve, and come up with strategies to work around their weaker areas. Coaches can help the members by providing the tools and frameworks they need to guide their reflective practice.

Designing an action plan is the follow-on step of the coaching process. An action plan is a concrete road map through which clearly identified goals are broken down into achievable steps, with each step detailing what to do, what resources it takes and when it should be done. It lays out the landscape in front of them and forces people to keep track. A sustainable action plan is one that benefits from regular check-ins and progress reviews, so any necessary adjustments can be made to keep everything relevant.

Coaches do not answer every question; instead, they help individuals to discover it. Empowerment includes encouraging self-reliance and breeding self-confidence. That means to celebrate the small successes and making sure that everyone continues to grow and get better. Coaching is a dynamic, ongoing process that changes to address the particular needs of unique beings.

However, success is granted to the pursuers of patience and persistence. You can't take on a new frame of mind overnight, and you must be content to slip up along the way. A good coach maintains (an abundance of) support and high-level perspective, a buffer from life that enables them to stay resilient and stay laser-focus on the long-term vision. Because of their successful coaching techniques, leaders can bring out the best in those they lead creating a culture that celebrates success and innovation.

Providing Constructive Feedback

Feedback is one of the most delicate instruments in a leader's toolbox. It starts conversations or shuts them down. It makes me realize when I have given feedback in the past — it actually has a huge effect on people. A leader has a higher purpose by design, to lead, to elevate, and help people grow... they are not meant for degrading.

The way I treated the feedback sessions only makes me cringe as I remember back to how I handled it as a new leader. I had a lot of fear to hurt someone's feelings or saying the wrong thing. I eventually came to learn that what makes feedback constructive has got far less to do with the content within the message and far more to do with how it is delivered and its underlying intentions. This is all about being honest with our kids while also showing compassion to ensure that we keep the other person feeling treasured and not targeted.

Some of the best lessons I learned was the How to time. Trying to give feedback in such an emotional climate will seldom have the effect we seek. What I learned: Patience is a virtue because if we both just stepped back and waited for the storm to let up, we could have engaged in much more productive conversation. This patience more often than not resulted in a more constructive conversation where the other party was less on the defense side and also much better invested.

But the actual crux is specificity. Abstract comments like "You need to get better" do not suggest direction.

I started getting more concrete and breaking down real examples of how actions lead to outcomes. This clarity helps the receiver understand what exactly to change and why. A comment like "Your reports are inadequate" was replaced with feedback on a report, specific areas that need work, and ways to improve it.

The hack in my situation was to always be prepared and connect the feedback you have to give with their larger goals/aspirations. Instead, feedback is directly tied to the growth and development of an individual which makes it a truly powerful source of empowerment rather than criticism. I usually begin by recognising the positives and what they have brought to the table, which sets up a positive foundation. This makes them quite confident as well, so they are open to criticism.

Enabling listening is another cornerstone of giving good feedback. It is more than just what I say but also the recipient's point of view. I make sure to encourage an open dialogue and ask for their perspectives. Through this dialog, many times they have given me pointers that I might not have caught. This kind of two-way communication also helps you to respect each other. It turns feedback into a conversation, or relationship, not something that is done "to" someone else.

The role of empathy in this process. Imagining what the recipient is going through helps me to understand the how much of an emotional impact my words really have. It is an exercise in compassion, for knowing everyone has their weight to carry. This has created a safe space where feedback is part of personal improvement, rather than judgment.

Finally, follow-up is critical. Offering feedback is not an event but a journey. I check in on my friends and make sure to support them, cheering loudly for every milestone. By staying in touch consistently, it also reinforces the connection that says I have a vested interest in their growth and success.

In retrospect, these experiences have become a soft of barometer to measure my development where feedback is concerned. What was once something that I was not looking forward to became a chance to try and encourage what could be there and help things improve. Constructive feedback is an art, one that epitomises the nature of thoughtful leadership — it requires using words with care and intent, delivering them in a way that both inspires and evokes growth.

Building a Mentorship Program

Most of us agree that mentorship is one the most powerful tools in our personal as well as professional growth kit. For me, the mentors who shared their time, guidance and listened when I needed it most came to mind reflecting on my experiences. Starting such a program within an institution is anything but aligning people; it is building a culture of development, encouragement and learning ongoing.

First, like many, the mentors that had a tremendous influence on me. But it was their impact beyond the boundaries of their advice that resonated — they immediately understood my unique challenges, dreams and overall mission. They made me see that while my immediate tasks were daunting, I had to think long-term and be strategic in investing for the future. Tsai answered, "Create real relationships that help people dig deep and unlock...the full essence of themselves.

Any mentorship program must be grounded on an understanding of what mentors or mentees really want from it. You must start with a concise sense of what the program is designed to deliver. Do we want to develop ourselves as stronger leaders, become more effective in our jobs, or grow personally in some way part of — their content? These objectives, in turn, will inform the format and content of the program. I am reminded of ... I know the term, emeritus actually means retired (smh), but my mentor was sort of like that still — hauling three four-lane highway traffic generation projects at once. Their input helped me both perform better and learn a great deal about how to tackle problems (and remain sane)

Another important step is the mentor selection part. The ideal mentors are skilled and, at the same time, human—full of empathy, patience and care for others. This isn't so much about hiring former senior managers with glossy resumes but finding people who can relate to their mentees on an individual level I recall a mentor who took out all time for our meeting even when he was super engaged. The dedication they had for me showed that they were not only financially in my success, but it also pushed me to work even harder both at school and continued to strive for more.

It is not just like fitting part A into slot B when it comes to matching mentors and mentees. Well, that has ALWAYS been the basis of a good work relationship. Think of general traits in the person you are sending a message out to, like personality, communication style and professional background. The most impactful mentorships I've had have all been rooted in a deep personal relationship. That bond permitted an easy flow of blunt honesty, an eternal component in the evolution of both sides.

After the program is established, consistency and evaluation are key. With regular check-ins, you can make sure relationships are going well and that both mentors and mentees are getting something from the experience. Ways like survey or a casual talk to assess the effectiveness of anything, what is serving well and where one has to correct it. One of the feedback sessions that I remember so well is when my mentor and me were speaking very openly regarding where we had moved to. This frank communication really helped us in refining our sessions and made the mentorship far more result oriented.

Designing a leadership coach Mentoring Program is an ongoing effort involving all stakeholders. An investment in people, a culture where knowledge is passed and growth instigated. I often think back at all the mentors I have had and it makes me think of how much influence they played on my life path. Their advice, encouragement, and belief in me has been critical to making me the leader I am today. Now is the time to use those best practices and traits, and create a mentoring program that teaches others so that we break down barriers for a future where everyone can learn, develop, and lead.

Success Stories

Success is a unique term for all of us, but leadership is a medicine which can help you to grow in spite of whatever situation you are going through. The following are stories of how young leaders accomplished embrace core principles that led them to success — and you can as well.

About Mia, a student balancing classes, internships and clubs. She was bombarded by it at first with all the pressure and high hopes. But she never turned back, and instead used her natural leadership abilities to make a difference. "Setting clear and attainable goals has to be the number one priority," Mia reveals how she streamlined the purpose of her campus club with open communication, and teamwork in mind. By creating an inclusive culture, Mia's club not only hit its targets but beat them — and she became the president. It also exemplifies how astute perspective and effective communication can change the game for leadership while leading the team.

And then there are the likes of Rohan, who created a side hustle while still in college. His startup saw some early struggles and he had to learn the hard way that success does not come overnight. But he didn't quit. He emphasized with his team and focused on self improvement, listened to feedback from his peer and users. Rohan shared that it was his job to make sure his team understand that when you fail, you learn. His startup began to gain traction and it soon far exceeded his original expectations. His journey illustrate us how Empathy, and Resilience are the reasons to ignite a path of success even after falling down.

A group centered on community service was headed by Amina, a student involved in a number of social causes. Notwithstanding constrained resources and interminable bureaucratic red tape, she stayed true to her mission. Her leadership was based on fundamental beliefs in fairness and inclusion, which inspired other to follow her. Amina was able to grow her group over time and make a real difference in the community. Her journey is evidence that we all have the ability to create change if we are driven by a deep conviction and practice an inclusive form of leadership, regardless of any barriers in our way.

Finally, let's go to Dylan who was the head of tech club occured during rapid growth at his school. Dylan led his team into unknown territory(new technology, priorities changing weekly, etc...) by focusing on continuous learning and adaptability. Their club was always at the bleeding edge of front office and administrative thought under his leadership, a pioneer in many respects. The platypus can teach us a lot about how adaptability and future-thinking are both key qualities a leader needs to demonstrate when things around them start looking more like molasses then water.

These stories provide important lessons on the type of vision, empathy, resilience and adaptability required to successfully lead – even while you are still in school. But it's not about having all the answers; true leadership is about learning, growing and leading with integrity, period. Using these principles you can do the same in your clubs, projects, or future career.

XV
Continuing Your Leadership Journey

Lifelong Learning

So much of the way I lead got formed as taught to me by all those teachers and experiences when I reflect on the idea of lifelong learning — it seems like my own private reality show! Oh please... Thinking that learning only happens in a classroom or via old dusty textbooks is for dinosaurs! I have now learned that true learning is like Instagram; it goes on and on, and the best kind happens outside of a classroom.

This idea of lifelong learning could not hold truer, especially in leadership. Being adaptable is one of the bedrock principles in being an effective leader regardless of the field or area you specialize in, whether it refers to business landscape shifts or societal growth movements. But the unifying factor behind this flexibility is our dedication to lifelong curiosity—our acceptance that no matter what we think we know, there is always still more to learn.

I look back on my own journey and I remember a key moment as a young professional. I had, barely out of school and armed with a fresh head full of text-book knowledge, and the boundless energy that comes with youthful enthusiasm, wanted to make my mark! But it was only a matter of time before I faced problems that textbooks did not explain how to address. That is when I first understood how valuable experiential learning was — learning based on trial and error, for one of you entrepreneurs out there!

The best leaders are the continuous learners. We are the ones who read, converse, listen far and wide. This is because everyone of them knows that every interaction can teach you something and helps us get better in everything. And, I think this is exactly the mindset that separates great leaders from average ones.

Today, lifelong learning has taken a fresh turn in the fast-moving world. The primary reason is simply because technology has changed the way we gain new information on a topic and learn. Most of those things can be pursued at your own pace with on-line courses, webinars,podcasts, and virtual conferences like never before. This wealth of information, however, poses the problem of separating signal from noise. This is where the need for critical thinking and discernment are called to improve from continuous learning and reflection.

Another important lesson, and a humbling one at that, is the importance of humility in learning. It can be easily to fall into the trap of thinking that we know it all and that how come everything "our way" because you may have some successes. But the best leaders are those who stay in wonder, who interrogate rather than assume, and who can be clear when they are perplexed. Not only does this kind of humility allow you to grow but also it forms an environment in which others feel valued and able to sharemore.

I have also realized in my leadership journey, how much I can learn from others. My personal growth has relied on both being a mentor and having mentors. Mentors have given me irreplaceable advice and being a mentor has expanded my understanding of potential ideas and has reinforced known insights. It is a symbiotic relationship between learning and leading.

As I think more about the heart and soul of lifelong learning, I recall that it is an activity of flux for life. It is about being curious, and open to new experiences, always looking to get better. It is understanding that leadership is not a place you reach, it is an eternal journey. It is most important to realize that learning the journey in itself is one of the biggest rewards of leadership.

Seeking New Challenges

Challenges are The Forge of Great Leadership While love hurts most of the times, in leadership it begins to matter that one only finds new trials and tribulations in order to find what all can be explored from within. Sometimes when I look back at my own path, the moments that produced the greatest anguish and suffering were often also most powerful change forces.

Years back I was in a position that I aced. The tasks of the day were almost mundane, the issues routine and the answers pretty much an automatic. So it was sort of cozy, on the outside. On the other hand, comfort is a deceptively dangerous place for anyone who wants to lead. It is pseudo security that suppress growth and innovation. I had realized I wanted to escape from this comfort zone even when one was finally happening.

When we challenge ourselves, it means we are going out there in the wilderness where there is no certainty outside. This unknown is an uncomfortable place to be, but in this no mans land learning really does occur. When I foolishly decided to work on something that was related to a field not of my own, I encountered words and landing right into some unfamiliar territory. At first, failure was my biggest fear. But with every challenge, I found an entirely new dimension of myself to explore and conquer. That project was groundbreaking for not only being successful (which made it unprecedentedly significant to me) but also because it expanded the boundaries of what I thought myself capable.

Finally, in leadership new challenges must not only be sought after but also promoted for others. A leader can guide, but also has to inspire. If I was willing to take risks and step into uncharted territories myself, then the team would see that too and know that growth is all about getting comfortable at being uncomfortable. I would often nudge team members toward roles or projects that were outside their comfort zone. Seeing them face these obstacles and come out the other side, more self-assured and able was a victory in itself.

Also, with new challenges come an environment that promotes a culture of continual growth. When a team is out together seeking and striving to tackle new challenges it breeds an environment of innovation and resilience. I can recall starting an initiative to have different departments come together and fix a long-standing problem. This was a big challenge because it required to break those silos and enable communication channels among teams that rarely spoke the same language. It was a very messy process involving miscommunications and conflicts, but it came to a transcendent conclusion. But more importantly, which created a better team that could now face the next challenge of life.

Looking back at each of these experiences, the true nature of seeking new challenges emerges as nothing more than a much trickier terrain to navigate. It is the story of character development and self-realization. Every obstacle that one faces and overcomes only fortifies their depth of leadership. Life is an ongoing school of experience — a process of learning, unlearning... relearning.

The journey of leadership is not linear, it consists of hills and valleys. Every challenge we face is a stepping stone to the next peak, another chance for meaningful transformation and to lead just that little bit wiser and more securely. Leaders can raise their own capabilities to new levels, always looking for the next challenge — an action that also helps set the framework for others to step up. Above all, that is what leadership is, a never ending quest for expansion.

Staying Motivated

Motivation is the invisible hand in our lives but also the light that guides us and makes us endeavor for the very best. Otherwise, the savviest of leaders can stumble and err amongst the numerous difficulties and obstacles which are par for the course in any endeavor. As I like to say, in thinking about my journey and all of the rest of this, it's not always about keeping a high but sailing on with grace through the lows.

Perhaps one of the most powerful lessons is based on connecting to your inner values. Motivation is the natural byproduct of aligning your actions with your deepest beliefs and principles. But Sometimes We Need To Step

Back And Remember What Really Matters. How do you align your day-to-day life with your larger, core values? If not, you might need to recalibrate. Such alignment not only energizes motivation but also leaves behind a more lasting sense of satisfaction than the mere pursuit of achievement.

The other key to continuous motivation is setting plain simple goals that can be met. As noble as big dreams are, they can also be terrifying. Then, breaking those larger mountains into smaller ones to set the road-map in such a way that it appears explicit. Every small triumph helps keep the body and mind moving forward by providing the build-up of wins necessary to feel like you are making headway. This is a practice grounded in self-compassion and foresight, understanding that the road to leadership is long —profitable, but certainly not instantaneous.

It cannot be overstated how important it is to be surrounded by a supportive and inspiring community. The people we cross paths with can either raise or destroy our vibration. Mentors, peers and even the subordinates which challenge you — that excite you. Through their eyes, you may see something you have never considered before and hearing "you got this" can reignite why you started in the first place. It is like standing in front of a mirror, seeing yourself and all that you are capable of (many times when it seems otherwise).

You need to have a growth mindset—Seeing hardship as learning, rather than barriers or advice to give up on something. That change in orientation is important to resilience, which helps us bounce back with a fresh charge. It is the attitude of being curious and relevant, unlike success-oriented or failure-orientated people who have their priorities defined.

Most people take it for granted, but self-care is crucial to keep the momentum going. The physical shape is related to the stability of the mind and emotions. Doing routine workouts, having enough sleep and practicing mindfulness techniques such as meditation or journaling to name just a few are all means of influencing how much energy we have at our disposal and by extention our ability to focus. It honors the leader as a whole person not just a role or a title with itself.

In the same way, thinking about all that you have achieved, little it is, can motivate to reach your goals. We are so just freaking busy with the hustle that we can miss our own progress. Such extract moments gives us a short glimmer of victory, which when celebrated strengthens our resolve to carry on. To break free of the chaos, it's about creating your own ash narrative so that when things get hard, you can remember what stands as a testament to success.

If we are going to remain motivated in the leadership arena, it must be done subtly and in stages. Such motivation is one that is sustained by aligning with our core values, setting clear goals, building a supportive community around us, staying in growth mindset mode as much as possible, and becoming conscious to prioritize self-care while celebrating the milestones we achieve along the way. The path is not linear and there are no quick fixes, but these are the approaches that turn it into an opportunity for joy and growth.

Reflecting on Growth

I was that naive kid who believed, Leadership is just like Mount Everest — very high up in the sky and needs oxygen tanks. Then I remembered that it is like a trek with a sprinkling of self-discovery, sort of like playing through a maze in games.

I have crossed the milestones—collected my Pokémon like they are some random cards which I am going to play in life but ironically that is just a bonus level. The real glow-up? It is something hidden and magical happening inside — a better version of yourself as though you have upgraded your character in video gaming. So cheers to all of the embarrassing moments and surprising lessons that shaped me into who I am killer-influence

My understanding of leadership was coloring through authority and position power at first. I believed a leader was someone who had all the answers and who could see out in front to navigate the ship. Except, as I navigated the role further, it was clear that leadership is just as much about hearing and following directions.

One thing that I most certainly had underestimated at the get-go, though, was how much actually being able to listen to other people — and have a grasp on their POVs and internal challenges!

There was resistance, at times within me and with those I led. These moments were pivotal. They made me question the way this whole thing is done, and forced me to change. Though it's difficult for me to realize that maybe my way is not always the best way, it had to be said. The two most important parts of that philosophy involve embracing mistakes and feedback. In fact, this vulnerability became our biggest asset by building trust and encouraging teamwork.

In addition, my leadership style has evolved as a result of the mentors and colleagues who have crossed my path. They had some great insights and criticisms. They were mirrors of my strengths but the reflection also showed me where I fell short. The greatest thing I discovered was the value of mentorship supporting you, but also being someone others could turn to. Not only was mentoring others a way for me to grow, it forced me to build the skills of explaining my thoughts and experiences in ways that were useful or insightful.

A huge part of my personal growth came at learning how to blend vision with execution. In my early days as a leader, I spend far too much time on big plans and audacious goals. This was good, but I realized that even if one is able to visualize, the next set of success factors is in breaking it down into implementable steps and ensuring high persistence & resilience on the journey. It was this pragmatic way of doing things which took firm hold among policy makers that speeches did not remain mere castles in the air but well thought through targets.

It trained me in empathy as well. Humanizing the experience and connections — empathizing with people, understanding their fears, hopes and goals was the great transformation. This was more than just driving performance but was about creating an environment where people felt recognised and cared for. The change from results focus to people center of excellence was transformational for the shifts in team dynamics and ultimate success.

When I think of these times in my life, it is easy to see that growth as a leader never ceases. This is a combination of self-awareness, learning and adaptation. Overcoming the challenges and learning from both success and failure are not mere stepping stones but components of the leadership tapestry.

At the heart of leadership is the willingness to change, to question, and to seek in order to understand oneself and others more deeply. It is really a process of reflecting and it's not where you end up, but more so the life-long journey.

Inspiring Others

Inspirer, Hear This: Attention Future Leaders!

If you think leadership means barking commands at people like a movie drill sergeant, then get the heck out of here. You serve as a DJ for motivational air (everyone in high spirits) and you are only selected to drop the beat getting all of us dancing.

If you want to inspire others, it needs to be genuine and personally-driven but with an element of showing the other person why your perspective matters more than a viral meme. Prepare to tap into those secret abilities and bring out the Legends in your squad!

For those who really want to motivate others, you must understand that being a leader is much more than just barking out orders or goals. At the level of alignment, it is about touching our work so powerfully to take others with us in uncovering something deeper in them. Inspiring others is rooted in being genuine, caring, telling a powerful story that speaks to the collective goals of the group.

Inspiration is built upon authenticity. Trust and Credibility: Leaders who are authentic AND transparent build trust. That means being vulnerable, owning up to failures and telling stories from your life that illustrate your values and beliefs. Leaders who live by what they say tend to have a larger impact in the lives of others because people are inspired by authentic, leading-by-example leaders. True leadership is about walking the walk, not just talking the talk. In this way, their actions always match what they say.

The second one is compassion. Working with a good understanding and open mind, acknowledging the emotions, needs, perspective from others ultimately leads to an inclusive support environment. The empathic leaders are good listeners and they care about others. It helps the employees understand what may be worrying when they feel by swapping shoes, and equips them to offer genuine support which staff experience more included. It is this bond that promotes loyalty and motivation.

Concise and compelling communications are also paramount. Leaders need to communicate a vision that is both inspiring and possible, but that can still move their team. The vision must be articulated in a manner that shows everyone is contributing and their individual work (yes, even the most mundane) is vital to accomplishing the grand collective goal. Telling stories can help with this. Leaders share their stories bringing the vision and values of the organization to life in a narrative that inspires and energizes their team.

Celebrate all those wins, no matter how small they are, because it will totally help keep the good vibes high and you feeling inspired! Recognition of both individuals and teams promoted a habit of gratitude through public acknowledgment, and incentivizes ongoing hard work and commitment. This acknowledgment should be genuine and tailored to the strengths and contributions of that person.

Inspiring others to be better happens when opportunities for growth and development are made available. Investing in each of your team members personal and professional development shows you are serious about helping them succeed now and into the future. It can include working to become a better mentor, providing more challenging work and fostering a culture of learning. When people see their leaders are interested in them and their advancement, they are more likely to feel inspired and motivated to give their best.

Wanna inspire people?Give them a mission–make your team workplace Avengers gang! People feel super pumped to show up when work feels like something more than just another cog in the royal blue endless email chain. Which makes having the same conversation over and over again relevant just as binge-watching is a real hobby. That coffee unifies those tactical activities to a more profound purpose. The leaders ensure that when they show up, we will not just for the free drink on Friday morning.

Ohh — and the most important ingredient for inspiration: realness, empathy and a bit of heart to hearts that acknowledge feelings. Add a dash of gratitude for the hustle and purpose that everyone is on board with, and you get an unstoppable squad ready to crush! That, my friends, is leadership realness.